I

As much as I hate to include a disclaimer in this book, the society we live in dictates I have to cover myself and tell you a few things up front about what you'll read.

- I will tell you to get out of debt by living on less than you make and behaving.

- I will tell you that you shouldn't have secrets from your spouse about money (or anything else for that matter, except maybe the pending Christmas gift for him/her).

- I will tell you some of the story about how Stacy and I communicate with money and how we have become completely debt free (including our home) shortly after I turned 31 and before Stacy's 30th birthday.

- I will share scripture from the Bible (you know, God's Holy Word).

- I will offer information on some legal issues relevant to money and debt.

If any of this stuff will offend you, I make no apologies for it, nor should you expect me to -- ever. You might as well stop reading because I'm not excited about any hate mail you may send me. I hope the content challenges you to reflect on more than the simple math of your financial situation.

I have a great deal of education and real-world experience behind the advice I'll share, and I mean every word I write. However (and here comes the cover myself part), I am not able to ensure that you will interpret my words with 100% accuracy, nor am I an attorney, a certified public accountant, a tax professional, a marriage/family counselor, a psychotherapist, a member of the clergy, or any other type of "professional" who is licensed or certified to offer a custom solution for your exact situation. Because I cannot possibly know the details of your situation, you should seek the counsel of a licensed professional to assist you if you have any concerns involving illegality or other major risks. I am responsible for opening your eyes about how to behave with your money–I am not responsible if you take that information and go do something stupid with it.

Contents

Introduction

Debt equals risk and there is no exception to that equation. I've said this phrase countless times over the past 15 years or so that I've been doing financial coaching, and the power of those words often gets overlooked. For those who grasp the power of the phrase when I say it to them, it is life-changing. For those who hear me but don't really grasp what I mean, the phrase has little impact on them, and I usually don't see them make any real positive changes to their financial situation. That's why I want you to see the phrase over and over again. **Debt equals risk and there is no exception to that equation.** Think about what that really means. Do you want risk in your life? Be careful how you answer.

It isn't a trick question, but the answer is **yes**, you **do** want risk in your life. Without risk, most of you wouldn't have a job or be driving a car or have thousands of other things. Without risk, nothing would ever get accomplished because risk is a necessary element of making any choice (or no choice at all). This is where we'll really spend some time in this book. You have choices to make, and every single choice you make has an associated risk. Despite what many people in our society say and what our government preaches, you do have a choice. Along with each choice, there is an associated risk. Economists will often refer to this risk as "opportunity cost." We'll get into that more in the forthcoming chapters, but simply put, your decision has implications because you chose Option A instead of Option B or, you chose not to act at all (which itself is a choice and has risks associated with it).

Here's the whole key to this book. Are you ready? You don't want lots of **unnecessary risk** in your life. You need to embrace the risks that are reasonable–and they are many! I know what you're thinking: "Barry, that's too broad a definition! What's reasonable?" Much of our legal system is built on answering that very question, and no two people will answer it the same way for every situation. In this book, I'll give you my thoughts on ways to minimize your unnecessary risks (especially those in your finances) based on my experience as a financial counselor and the things I've learned personally along the way.

I recognize there are people out there who live for taking risks and who thrive on the rush it brings when a big risk pays off. If you're reading this book and fit into that category, you're probably going to disagree with some of what you'll read. That's okay–stick with me–maybe I can challenge your thinking and drive you to become even bolder in your steps toward getting out of debt and building wealth for your family.

Then there are those on the other side of the spectrum. Any risk paralyzes you. You can't make a decision because you're always sure it is the wrong one. You look at every possible outcome (even those that are so unlikely a drunken gambler in Vegas wouldn't even consider betting on it) and agonize over what it could mean for you. You are so risk-averse that even reading the previous paragraph made you sweat. If you're reading this book and fit into that category, don't give up on me either! You'll find recommendations in here that will challenge your thinking because you'll probably think them too dangerous or bold. Make baby steps. Don't try to overdo it, but realize that if you really want to change you must make a choice to change.

At the end of most chapters, I'll give you some action steps and questions to consider that will help you internalize the key concepts from that chapter. Are you ready to begin the journey to finding out how to knock out your debt and recognize the freedom that comes from having no payments? Let's get started!

Chapter 1:
Debt Defined

Although it may seem to be a silly starting point, I want to spend a few paragraphs defining what debt really is. I want us to start on the same page when it comes to debt, which should help us as we get into the discussions of different types of debts. Webster's dictionary defines debt as "an obligation or liability to pay or return something; the condition of owing." I suspect that nothing in that definition really surprises anyone who reads it. Let me expand a little on it for you. My expanded definition of debt is: "an obligation (responsibility, commitment, liability) by a borrower to pay money to someone (a lender, a creditor)."

As you read through Webster's definition and my expanded version, did it make you feel a little uneasy? If so, maybe it is because you've found lenders difficult to deal with. Maybe you've watched as someone's marriage fell apart because they couldn't handle the stress of being unable to meet the obligation of debt. Maybe you are like me and have seen both sides–someone with no debt and someone with lots of it–and are pretty sure you know which one you want to model your life after. Maybe you are familiar with the biblical passage found in Proverbs 22:7: "The rich rules over the poor, and the borrower is the slave of the lender" (ESV) and have lived it out. In other words, maybe you are a slave to your debt and are tired of it!

Debt is a very simple concept. You borrow money, promising to pay it back at a later time. The arrangement has been going on this way for generations–money gets borrowed, money gets paid back. That seems simple, right? The math is also very simple. You pay interest on whatever you borrow, usually as a percentage of how much you owe. The terms associated with debt–terms such as "principal," "APR," and "amortization"–are fairly common and are thrown around all the time when people are talking about debt. Most people have lots of debt, so it seems "normal" for you to go out and get a lot of debt, too. The attitude "I can afford the minimum payments, so I'm okay" abounds.

Starting from a very young age, you're expected to live in a nice house and drive a new car because everyone around you does. You do everything you can to avoid becoming one of "those people"–the ones who look destitute, living like they can't even afford to give their kids a bath. They drive old beat-up cars and live in houses that look like they haven't been cleaned since the 70s when the shag carpet was installed. They mow their yard once a year when the city threatens to haul them to jail if they don't, and random strangers often stop by their house on weekends because it looks like they're having a yard sale. Since you don't want to live like "those people," you go way too far in the other direction, racking up ridiculous debt along the way and perpetuating the lie that you have to live with lots of debt and you have to have lots of stuff early on in life when you have no business buying it.

As Larry Burkett noted, most young couples attempt to live like their parents immediately after getting married. The problem with this attempt is that their parents are 25 years ahead of them in accumulating that stuff. Don't get me wrong. I want you to live in a nice house, drive a nice car or two, and have nice stuff. I just don't want you to do it at the expense of your sanity. I want you to live a life so that people recognize you as just a little weird because you aren't so worried about money. I want you to pay off your house early and avoid stupid financial decisions so you don't go to work every day just to pay payments to some bank. That is absolutely no fun. Instead, I want you to realize that money is only a tool for you to manage and use. I want you to understand that debt is not a tool, as I was told it was all through business school, but more appropriately should be treated like a coiled rattlesnake ready to bite you if you make a misstep. In other words, I want you to move from debtor to better!

Before you can get there, you need to understand the root of most financial problems–lack of discipline and/or ignorance. Most Americans are so personally involved with debt without having any knowledge of how the math really works and/or what the full implications of debt are. They don't understand how it is possible to pay the same credit card bill for 15 years and still owe on it. They don't understand why they can never seem to pay off one car before they "need" another one. Since schools generally do a terrible job of teaching students how to take care of their finances, and since parents often do a horrible job of managing their own finances, what more can we expect? If you've never been taught how to handle money properly, why is it reasonable for anyone to expect you to know how?

Since you spent the money to buy this book, you are obviously ready to make a change in your financial life. I hope to provide you with all the tools you need to get started on your education of how to move from debtor to better. Unfortunately, though, I can't change your behavior. I can only give you the necessary information to equip you. You have to decide you want to change. If you're already in debt, what do you have to lose by learning the principles in this book and giving them a try?

If you haven't fallen prey to debt, don't you want to avoid the pitfalls associated with it? It is still up to you. My job in these pages is to arm you with the necessary knowledge on how debt works and how you can get out of it. Your job is to take action. So get to it!

Action Steps:

1. Write my expanded definition of debt on a blank sheet of paper, highlighting or underlining the terms "obligation," "borrower," and "lender."". On the same sheet, write down the text to Proverbs 22:7. Post this sheet somewhere you will see it regularly.

2. Think about a time when you did something *really stupid* with your money. Write down that event and some thoughts about why you now know it was such a bad idea.

Chapter 2:
Looking Back to
See the Significance

I'm glad I haven't scared you off yet. You are taking a risk reading this book. You risk changing your view and perception of debt and the risks you take with your money, and some of you are even risking a meal because funds are so tight you had to choose between buying this book or buying some groceries. There are many things left to learn, and if you've been with me this far, either you are intrigued enough to face your fears about debt and learn how to deal with them or I've made you mad enough that you have to keep reading so you can send me a nasty email about how wrong I am. Either way, we're in this together.

Before we go any further, take a few minutes and complete the following exercise. Think for a moment about the past ten years of your life. In the space below, I want you to write the top three most significant events that have happened to you in the past ten years (good or bad):

1. _____

2. _____

3. _____

Now, I want you to review those events and jot down a few notes about why those events were so significant:

_____

_____

_____

_____

As you review your notes above, think about what you could have done (if anything) to change those events: Jot down those thoughts below.

_____

_____

_____

_____

If the event(s) was a negative experience, what actions could you have taken to avoid or minimize the negative impact of the event(s)?

_____

_____

_____

_____

If the event(s) was positive, what actions could you have taken to make more of the experience and maximize the positive impact of the event(s)?

_____

_____

_____

_____

In this exercise, most people will list things such as the death of a spouse, bankruptcy, major illness, and the like as the significant event. Others will jot down something such as marriage, a major promotion, graduation from school, or the birth of a child. No matter what you listed, I want you to answer one final question about these events. What was the monetary impact of those events? In other words, what happened to your bank account as a result of the events you listed?

_____

_____

_____

_____

I hope you spent some time on this exercise because it will help you internalize the reality that most significant life events have a major financial implication. Unfortunately, many times the financial aspect of an event turns out to have the longest-lasting impact on your life. For example, if you listed the death of a spouse as one of your significant events, you likely experienced some or all of the following financial implications of that event as well:

- Loss of income
- Funeral/burial costs
- Redoing your household budget
- Food/diet changes
- Insurance policy changes
- Hospital/hospice costs
- Automobiles and housing (sell one or buy something different)

Look again at the list above. Each of the items in this example represents hundreds (maybe thousands) of dollars, not to mention the huge emotional toll associated with handling the loss of your soul mate.

The point of this entire exercise is to put you in the right frame of reference to discuss risk and how to embrace the appropriate level of risk in your financial life based on you, your situation, and your income. The very first booklet I wrote on personal finance is titled *It's Not About Money* because the truth is, personal finance is not about money. It is about behavior. It is about priorities. It is about maturity. It is about defining your comfort level with risk and acting accordingly. It is not about money. Don't get me wrong: money comes into play in this discussion because this is, after all, a personal finance book. The focus, however, is on things other than money. Visit *http://bit.ly/1Ekgeoy* if you'd like a free copy of *It's Not About Money* for yourself

Here's the scary part of all the things I've had you looking at so far in this chapter. If you look forward ten years, you likely will experience another significant event or two that will overshadow the event(s) you listed above. You cannot avoid many of the major events in your life. Something will happen to you. My goal is to help you be more financially prepared so you can deal with the event and move on. Let's look at it another way, through an example.

When our daughter Annie was born, we had a pretty good idea it was going to cost some money. I don't think doctors just graduate from med school and receive a Porsche and a mansion along with their diploma. My brother-in-law is a doctor, and that's not how it worked for him. Doctors study hard, work hard, and expect good payment for their services. I think this is fair and valid, and I want to be able to pay for the services they offer. I didn't even do well in high school biology–you don't want me as your doctor. So when we found out Stacy was pregnant, I had no plans of making that a DIY project. In fact, it never crossed my mind. I simply knew I would pay a doctor (and a crew of other medical professionals) to handle it for us.

When we learned of the pregnancy, we knew we had about eight months before Annie would arrive. Many people in that situation start celebrating and having fun with the process of pregnancy, completely overlooking the fact that hospital bills and other expenses are headed their way to go with that new bundle of joy. Thankfully, we were well-grounded in reality and started making some phone calls. I called the insurance company, the doctor's office, and the hospital to ask them how much everything was going to cost. Yes, I know this points out how big of a nerd I really am, but it helps prove my point, so stick with me. We broke down the cost into an amount we could save monthly so we would be able to pay cash for the whole thing. In other words, we made a plan. When we went to doctor's appointments, we paid cash. When we got the hospital bill, I called and paid in full and got a hefty discount for doing so. Our behavior (financially) allowed this major life event to occur without negative financial implications. We didn't have to pay payments on our baby. When she came home, she was fully ours as God's gift to us. We have enjoyed the births of two new little ones since that initial experience and followed the same plan each time. It is much easier to attend to baby's needs when you don't have to worry about making payments for the costs associated with bringing home this new bundle of joy.

Here's my point–life will happen. You will have unexpected expenses. But how many of those unexpected expenses are big surprises simply because you simply didn't have a plan? Be honest. Many people argue this with me, and I'll admit they do make one salient point. How can you have a plan for something you don't know is going to happen? How can you plan for the unexpected? Well, I'm glad you asked. Let's talk next about the answer.

Action Steps:

1. Go back and review your exercises from this chapter. Make any additional notes that will help you clearly define what significant events have shaped your life in recent years.

2. What is your motivation for getting out of debt? Dan Miller, author of 48 Days to the Work You Love, says that if you can tell someone why you want to do something, you can often figure out the how.

Chapter 3:
Getting Started:
Breaking the Cycle

*"...not doing anything is its own decision,
and the odds of failure are horrible."*

–Jon Acuff

If you've ever talked with me about money, you know that this is the part of the book where I'm going to talk about an emergency fund. I want to get this out of the way early on so you can understand how we can avoid those speed bumps along the way from being a debtor to truly becoming better. Let's start by spending a few minutes going over what an emergency fund is and, just as importantly, what an emergency fund is not.

At some point in your life, you are going to have to deal with a country music scenario. You know what I'm talking about–your wife leaves, your dog dies, your truck breaks down–and of course it all happens on the same day. This scenario leaves you with two options–move to Nashville and write a hit song about it to cover all the expenses you just incurred or figure out another way to pay for all that mess–and figure it out fast! Since most of you probably aren't going to be ready to write a hit song, let's assume you have to jump to plan B–an emergency fund–without Nashville as an option.

An emergency fund (you may also hear it called a "rainy day fund") is a sum of money set aside for when those country music scenarios come along. Most people live their lives in denial of a financial emergency ever happening to them, but face it–you are going to have something happen to you that you won't expect. It will have a financial implication and it will happen when you really don't want to deal with it. Having a buffer against financial problems is one of the most important places to start down the path toward financial success. Without a financial shield against emergencies, any personal disaster will likely result in a massive negative financial shock wave that will continue long after your personal disaster.

If you're a worrier, an emergency fund will also let you sleep better at night. It will make your spouse happier, and both of you will be a lot less worried about financial issues in general–all because you have a cushion in case something happens.

An emergency fund must be something you can access quickly, easily, and without causing yourself any major harm. In its simplest form, an Emergency Fund is a savings or money market account, separate from all your other accounts. It should be easy enough to access that you can get to it but not so easy that you don't have to think about whether your financial "emergency" is really an emergency or just a little hiccup. One good way to make sure your emergency funds are safe and not a temptation is to open a savings account at a bank separate from the one where you keep your other accounts. When setting up the account, don't set up online banking, and don't get any check-writing privileges. This basically means that any time you feel there is a financial emergency, the only way to access the money is to physically get in the car, drive to that bank, and walk in to make a withdrawal. This may sound like overkill, but if you don't have the discipline to stay away from your emergency fund unless there is a real emergency, this is an easy way to help instill that discipline. While we're at it, let me be clear that a credit card is not an Emergency Fund. A bunch of jewelry or baseball cards or anything else you could sell (even if you think you could sell it quickly) is not an emergency fund. An emergency fund is cash (or a true cash equivalent).

The next obvious concern is to determine how much you should save in your emergency fund. Since every person is different, I can't tell you how exactly much you need to set aside, but I can give you a suggestion that will help you figure it out for yourself. Ready? Here it is: Start with one paycheck. Most studies show that a staggering number–about 70%–of Americans live paycheck to paycheck. That means taking this one step in your financial plan will put you at the financial fitness level of the top 30% of Americans! Most people have nothing saved and no plan for what to do if something goes wrong. Think about it–without any savings, you're as little as 2-3 weeks from being unable to pay any bill that comes in, including the necessities such as food and electricity. If your income stopped today, how long would you make it?

Dave Ramsey promotes seven "baby steps" as his plan for getting you out of debt and on track to build wealth. His very first baby step is to save $1,000 as a starter emergency fund while you are paying off debt ($500 if your household take-home pay is less than $20,000 per year). This recommendation is to give you a hedge against needing to go back into debt if something comes up. I think this is generally good advice, but after counseling hundreds of people who make very little, and others who make quite a lot, I've found this is not a good one-size-fits-all solution. Instead, I want you to start by setting a goal of saving the amount of one of your regular paychecks. If you are on a very small income and/or have very small ongoing expenses, $1,000 may be way too much for you to be able to save in a short period of time. Conversely, if you have a huge income and extremely high ongoing expenses, $1,000 may be too little. A single paycheck will keep you from living in expectation of that very next check just to keep yourself afloat. I know it will take time, but I have also witnessed firsthand the power of having this buffer against a financial crisis.

I beg you to get out of the "waiting for payday" mentality. I want you to have enough for an emergency and at the same time break the cycle of living paycheck to paycheck. While it won't keep you safe from emergencies that come with huge price tags, if you can get even one paycheck ahead it does three powerful things:

1. It starts you in the habit of saving.
2. It gives you a customized amount for saving based on your individual situation.
3. It allows you to prove to yourself that you really can do it.

I don't want you to take long to save this money. I want you to get a quick win under your belt because the longer it takes you to set aside this money, the less likely you are to feel as though you can do it. So don't waste time getting this money together. If saving this money means working extra hours for a month or two, having a yard sale, or putting some stuff from the garage onto Craigslist to make a little extra, do it. I don't want this step in your financial plan to take more than 2-3 months. Get some money saved and you'll be ready to say goodbye to the use of credit cards and other forms of "easy money" if/ when something comes up as you're trying to move to the next step of financial success–tackling debt. We'll spend more time on that soon.

By the way–and I know it may scare you a bit for me to share this now, but I'll chance it — once you've saved one paycheck, set a goal that once you are out of debt, you will save six months' worth of expenses as your granddaddy "I can tackle just about anything that will come up" emergency fund. I know this is a big goal, and one that won't come quickly for most. I don't care how much debt you are in, I want you to set your sights on becoming financially independent and ready for almost any emergency. Don't misinterpret me here–I don't want you to stop paying on your debts and work three extra jobs to save up six months of expenses at this point. I just want you to know that having this bigger sum in a savings account somewhere as a hedge against short-term financial emergencies is your ultimate goal.

Okay, I hope that didn't bring you to tears and you're ready to continue in this discussion. Let's talk about one last thing regarding the emergency fund. Many people are tempted to skip over this part of their financial plan and go straight into attacking their debt with a vengeance. Please don't! Having an emergency fund in place is what will keep you from losing your motivation when you've paid off most of your debt and then are hit with a big unexpected bill. I don't want you to have to go back to the very beginning and start all over again. An emergency fund will help keep you from falling on your face when something comes up and will instead show you that you can avoid relying on debt to make it in life and that you don't have to be "rich" to do it. Remind yourself how great it will be not to have to rely on that very next paycheck just to put food on the table.

Let me also give you one warning. The moment you make your commitment to save some income toward an emergency fund, you are going to have an "emergency."

I just want to put that out there because I don't want you to get mad at me when it happens. I promise it is not my fault! I think it is God's way of helping you learn the lesson of perseverance and determination. I think it is a test of whether you are really committed to making your money behave. So when you start saving and immediately have to have your car towed and spend $1,500 for repairs, don't blame me. Just know it is going to happen. Take on this monster with the same efforts you put forth to save up the emergency fund and then get on with things. Don't be discouraged by setbacks because they will be temporary. I don't want you to give up on trying to succeed with your money just because you had an unexpected expense and had to go back to your credit card because the cash to fix it wasn't there. Just keep at it and you will eventually succeed. It will take time, it will take effort, and most of all it will take discipline. In fact, discipline is the key to making this whole thing work. We'll talk about that in the next chapter.

Action Steps/Questions

1. Write down at least five ways you can make some extra money in the next two weeks. Make sure they're legal and moral, and make sure you can have cash in hand in two weeks.

_____

_____

_____

_____

_____

2. Pray for protection for yourself, your family, and your stuff as you make the commitment to start saving and begin the journey from debtor to better.

Chapter 4:
The Key to Making This
Whole Thing Work

"Recipes don't make cookies."
    –Sam Horn

Let me be blunt. Most people are simply too lazy to set aside a sum of money for emergencies or other big expenses. It isn't that they can't do it; they're just not willing to do it. I'm not going to be that annoying infomercial that tells you there are three simple steps to solving all your life's problems with money. Instead, I want to make it plain and simple that this isn't hard, but you won't do it if you don't understand and internalize the one big element to financial success where most people perform terribly–discipline.

Discipline will make all the difference. If you can say "no" to a few things and "yes" to a few others, you can be filthy stinkin' rich (for those of you who are not sure, filthy stinkin' rich is a couple of notches above plain old filthy rich). It really is that simple. Let me put this in perspective for you by way of an example. If I set up an account in your name and deposited $100,000 in it that would become yours in five years, you'd be very interested in knowing what strings were attached for you to be able to collect, right? Okay, here are the two strings for our example:

1. You have to come up with $10,000 cash in hand within 90 days. You don't have to give any of it to me, but you have to prove to me that you came up with at least that much cash.

2. You can't borrow any money to get the $10,000.

With those constraints, I bet 95% of you would find a way to come up with $10,000, right? Why? Because doing so would become important to you. You would recognize the value of scraping together $10,000, even if it meant sacrificing, doing extra work, and maybe even selling some things you decide you could live without for five years. You'd recognize that the value of having $10,000 cash in hand equals getting $100,000 in five years. The math is easy, and you'd be foolish not to do it, right?

What I really want to leave you with about the concept of discipline is this: Your decisions with money all boil down to deciding what is important to you based on a good healthy dose of reality, and then acting accordingly. Unless there is a math problem in your financial situation (where your required expenses consistently exceed your income), it all boils down to having the discipline to recognize and act upon the things you deem to be important and having the discipline to say "no" to the stuff that doesn't fit.

Let's look at it another way. If I gave you exactly $100 to spend on groceries that must last for two weeks, you would have to decide and prioritize which of the things on your list are necessary (needs), which are things you enjoy (wants), and which are things you enjoy but are probably too expensive to purchase given your budget (wishes). Selecting items to place in your cart based on these simple criteria forces you to make a financial decision, and since I only gave you $100 to work with, you have to exercise discipline to ensure you didn't purchase too little food and thus risk starvation.

For the entire process of personal finance to work, you must be willing to exercise sufficient discipline to make your income cover your expenses and, as long as it does, to always keep that equation in check. If the math doesn't work, you have to do something about it. The math of a budget is pretty finite. The formula is always:

INCOME - SAVINGS - EXPENSES = 0

You won't change the math unless you change your behavior, and that takes discipline–sometimes quite a lot of it. Discipline has gotten a bad reputation as something that isn't good for us and only hurts, but this reputation is undeserved. Hebrews chapter 12 even discusses the concept of discipline and how important it is, culminating in a verse that may prove useful here: "No discipline seems pleasant at the time, but painful. Later on, however, it produces a harvest of righteousness and peace for those who have been trained by it" (Hebrews 12:11 NIV). This Bible passage along with many of our life experiences serve as excellent evidence that although no one enjoys the process of developing discipline, it is truly necessary for us to succeed with our finances, with our relationships, and even with our willing submission to God. You must develop discipline to make this whole thing work.

How do you harness the power of discipline in your finances? I'm glad you asked. We'll look at that subject next.

Action Steps/Questions

1. Was it a revelation to you that I identified discipline as the key to making this whole money thing work? Why or why not?

2. List five ways you can instill discipline into your financial situation immediately. Once listed, put them into action!

_____

_____

_____

_____

_____

Chapter 5:
Make Your Money Behave:
The Scary B-Word

You knew this topic would come along eventually. You secretly hoped there was another way, but alas, it is time to discuss the dreaded B-word–budget. Budgets have gotten a bad reputation for telling you what you cannot do. This is wrong! Budgets, or more appropriately, Cash Flow Plans (I will use the terms budget and cash flow plan interchangeably from here on out), allow you to be in complete control of your money.

A household budget should be prepared once a month, every month, recognizing that each month is different. There are no stone tablets here–a budget isn't the same every single month. The gift budget for December is likely a little different from the gift budget for January, right? So you can't just do your budget and think it is a once-in-a-lifetime event.

Cash Flow Plans are not designed to keep track of where you spent your money; they are designed to help you prepare to spend your money based on what you deem most important for your family's needs that month. Again borrowing from Dave Ramsey, a correctly-created Cash Flow Plan allows you to "spend" every dollar (on paper) before the month begins, before you receive your first paycheck. Then, all you have to do is execute that plan. You are in complete control, and very little (if anything) will surprise you once you've established your plan and have gotten into the groove of managing your household finances. That last sentence is critical to understanding that you won't just put together a budget and magically have no financial problems. Your first budget won't work because you'll forget to include something really obvious such as groceries or your electric bill–oops. It'll take you a few months to get it all down. Like a toddler learning to walk, you'll make a few mistakes and feel a little silly at first. Stick with it–I promise it works itself out in a few months.

I regularly hear people complain about budgeting and how difficult it is. Budgeting is perceived as difficult for a few reasons:

• You are forced to make priorities that are based on reality.
• Discipline is required to stick to the plan.
• Every month (and thus every budget) is different.

Look at the reasons listed above. Are these bad things? Is it bad to prioritize in life, to have discipline, or to plan for change? It may not be the easiest thing to do, but once you have a workable budget, you will find there are also some really big reasons for sticking to it. Below are just a few:

• Planning for how to spend your money reduces the stress of the unknown.
• If you are married, making a budget significantly increases communication with your spouse.
• Budgeting increases your organizational and problem-solving skills.

Why wouldn't you want less stress, better communication, and better organizational and problem-solving skills? Let's look at the process of making a budget that really works.

A workable (read simple) budget is a bit of a science and a bit of an art. I promise that if you begin budgeting and it works the very first time, you did something wrong. On the flip side, if you begin budgeting and it hasn't started to really click within three or four months, you did something wrong. Usually the problem is that we want to over-complicate and account for every penny in our budget. This may be necessary for big corporations and our accountants, but in personal finance, it is simply unneeded. A successful budget will tell you (and anyone who may look at it) four things:

1. How much money do I have coming in for the month?
2. How much and how often am I setting aside money for emergencies and retirement?
3. What are my ongoing monthly expenses (rent/mortgage, utilities, gas, groceries, etc.)?
4. What are my major debts and how am I repaying them?

In other words, a budget shows what your priorities are! You've probably heard it said that you can tell what a person cares about by looking at his checkbook. There is one warning I need to provide on this–a budget is only a tool. Like any other tool, it can only help you succeed in completing a task; it cannot do the task for you. You will not succeed with a budget if you do not use it, and you will not use it if you make it too complicated. Let me say that again: You will not succeed with a budget if you do not use it, and you will not use it if you make it too complicated. Although some of you who read these words have a complicated financial mess (if this is you, consider the following pages and then seek out assistance from a competent financial counselor; contact me if you'd like an appointment or a recommendation), most of you have a very workable situation; you've just been too lax in your approach to personal finance.

Before You Start

Making a budget does not need to be complicated, but it does need to be organized. First, I will refer you to a few worksheets found in the Appendix of this book. If you're reading this digitally, you may want to consider printing those pages to have alongside the text you're reading here. If you're reading this in printed form, you are welcome to copy as many pages of any section of the Appendix of this book for yourself without worrying about copyright infringement. Second, you should spend some time compiling a complete "picture" of your income and bills each month. Why monthly? Because typically you're only going to get one electric bill, rent/mortgage bill, water bill, phone bill, etc., per month. When you get paid may differ from someone else, but I bet 99% of you get most of your bills only once per month.

To get an accurate picture of your monthly income, go look at old pay stubs and/or bank deposit records. You need to know with clarity how much income you're working with, focusing strictly on take-home (net) pay. Those of you who have a variable income (a commission-based salesperson, for example) can still get a good idea of your expected income for the next month (remember, with a budget every month is different) by looking back and compensating for changes since that previous pay period. Whatever amount you decide as your income to budget from, simply know that if you put too much (overestimate) you may have to play catch up somewhere on your expenses because you said you'd have more money than you actually got.

You also need to know some details about your expenses. How much is your mortgage/rent? How much do your utilities run each month? What other bills do you have (including credit cards, medical bills, and anything you don't pay every month such as taxes or insurance)? Once you have compiled all this information, you should set aside at least an hour to complete three worksheets in the Appendix at the back of this book: the Income Sources Worksheet, the Irregular Bills Worksheet and the Monthly Bills Worksheet. Don't worry–completing these sheets is something you only have to do once! Once you have completed them, you will need to update them only periodically as your situation changes.

Once you complete these worksheets, you are ready to make your first Cash Flow Plan/Budget (see Appendix). You should make a new cash flow plan every month, before the month begins. I also recommend keeping the cash flow plan once the month ends so you can use it as a future reference. Once you've compiled all the necessary information, let's get started!

Income Sources Worksheet

This sheet has many lines and you should not expect to fill all of them! Simply fill in the various forms of income you receive, how often you receive them, and what that amounts to on a monthly basis. If you are on a variable income, this is where you need to really consider how much you take home each month and commit to bringing home at least that much! Somehow, some way you are getting paid, and you just need to boil it down to an amount you are confident you'll bring home every month. If you aren't exactly sure, always underestimate.

In other words, if you think you'll make about $2,500 this month, but might only make $2,100, use $2,100. We'll talk about what to do with the extra money if/when it comes in.

You should enter all the income information in terms of your net income (what you take home after taxes and other pay deductions). Ultimately, the Income Sources Worksheet will tell you your monthly take-home income. For example, let's assume your household only has a single income source, a paycheck of $1,200 (take-home pay) that you receive on the 15th and 30th of each month. In this example, you would fill in $1,200 SALARY 1 AMOUNT field, list it is received on the 15th and 30th in the HOW OFTEN field, and list $2,400 in the MONTHLY field. At the bottom right of the page, you would list that you have $2,400 total monthly income.

Remember, if you have an irregular income, you should list that income in terms of what you commit to receive (not what you hope to receive but a reasonable expectation of what you will receive). If needed, look back at previous pay stubs to see how much you "normally" make. Also remember that it is always better to underestimate your income than to overstate it because this income is what you will have to use to pay your expenses.

Once you have completed the Income Sources Worksheet, set it aside. You will use it a bit later.

Irregular Bills Worksheet

This sheet, like the Income Sources Worksheet, has many lines and you should not expect to fill them all. Use the Irregular Bills Worksheet to list only those things that you don't pay every month. Usually, as the categories on the sheet indicate, this is some sort of tax or insurance payment or savings toward the repair or replacement of a large ticket item (such as a car, house roof, etc.).

To complete the Irregular Bills Worksheet, first fill in the total amount of each applicable category (life insurance annual premium, car insurance premium, etc.) in the AMOUNT column. Second, write in how often each bill is due in the HOW OFTEN column. Third, determine the monthly amount needed based on how often this bill is paid and write it in the MONTHLY column. This will tell you how much you need to set aside each month to ensure you're not surprised when an annual tax bill arrives, for instance. Instead, you should be prepared because you have set aside 1/12th of that amount each month in your budget.

I know I've gone a bit overboard on some of the items on this worksheet for some of you, but just fill in the lines that apply to you. As an example, when I wrote the first edition of this book I lived in Tennessee, in a county without a wheel tax or any other kind of ongoing vehicle fees except tag renewal. Tags were $24 per year and so I just cash flowed $24 the month they were due rather than put it on this form and set aside $2 per month. Remember the K.I.S.S. Principle here–don't make it any more complicated than it has to be! And for those of you who are looking for a rule of thumb on when to include or not include something on here–if it is something that costs more than $100 per year ($50 per year if you're on a very low income), include it. Otherwise, just adjust your budget in the month that item is due to cover the expense and move on.

Once you have completed the Irregular Bills Worksheet, set it aside. You will use it a bit later.

We have saved the easiest (in some ways, the hardest in others) of the worksheets for last. The Monthly Bills Worksheet captures all of the bills you pay every month such as rent/mortgage, electricity, water, phone, etc. Unlike the other worksheets, this one does not have any listed categories. My hope is that you pulled together all your bills as suggested in the Before You Start section to help you write in each of your monthly expenses. If you have not yet done that, please do so before continuing.

To complete this worksheet, write the name of the organization/person in the BILL column. For instance, if you have a mortgage through ABC Bank, you could write "mortgage" or "ABC Bank (house)". It is only important that you identify the bill. In the AMOUNT column, enter how much the bill runs each month. Some bills will vary from month to month so you can only estimate how much it will be. Just like the Income Sources Worksheet for those with a varying income, it is important that you enter a reasonable amount based on what you expect the bill to be. Of course, you probably won't be exact on your amounts, but you should be as close as possible, always overestimating rather than underestimating. In the DUE DATE column, list the date on which the bill is due each month. Do not include any grace period; list the actual due date. Of course, things such as gas and food won't have a due date. List the due date only for things that have one. Also, hopefully you are able to set aside something for yourself as savings.

In the NOTES column, list any information relevant to the bill. If it is a bill with a balance that will (you hope) go away eventually (such as credit card debt, medical bills, car loans, etc.) put the balance in the NOTES column. Please don't leave that part out–it is important!!! Having this information will help you as you prioritize your bills when/if there is extra income and/or if there is a bill that can't be paid this month because there isn't enough income to cover everything for some reason.

Don't forget to include the total of the irregular bills from your completed Irregular Bills Worksheet. There is a field for this at the bottom of the form and you don't want to miss it.

Once you have completed the Monthly Bills Worksheet, you should review it along with the Irregular Bills Worksheet to make sure you've covered all of the expenses you incur each month. Don't forget such things as food, entertainment, gas, etc. It may be helpful to go back and look over your previous months' bills as you complete this part of the budgeting process. If you look at this and are a little overwhelmed by what you see, don't be discouraged!

Summing it up Before We Move On

If you've followed my instructions up to this point, you should have three completed worksheets: the Income Sources Worksheet, the Irregular Bills Worksheet, and the Monthly Bills Worksheet. You can now breathe a big sigh of relief because the hardest part of this whole process is over. Until you have a major change in your situation (income or expenses), you don't have to go through these steps again. The part you do every month is much easier– and much less time-consuming. I guess what I'm trying to say is–if you've made it this far, don't give up! You're almost there.

Before you move on to the actual budget, I want you to stop for a few minutes and clean up whatever mess you've made around you. To do your budget, you need only a few things:

- A pencil with a decent eraser
- A calculator (or a good brain for math)
- The three worksheets you just completed
- A blank Cash Flow Calendar (see Appendix)
- A blank sheet or two of paper

Be sure to clear away any other papers and put away all other distractions. This includes children who are too young to understand this process and will only pull you away from it. This means you either need to have a babysitter for a bit or wait until the little ones are down for a nap or bedtime. If you're married, this could be a possible date night. Picture it with me–the romantic evening begins with husband and wife cheerfully discussing how their finances are headed toward the edge of a cliff. Be careful, though, or it might turn into one of those blame-game "discussions." You have to understand and be aware that any other paperwork, noise, or other issue (including being tired) will keep you from doing your best with this. If you'll give this process your best effort each month for a few months, you'll get the process down well enough that it will become a simple habit, and you'll never have to stress over it again. With that said, let's move into the actual monthly budgeting process.

Cash Flow Calendar

Once you have captured your income and expenses on all the previously-outlined worksheets and gotten together all the items I mentioned above, it is time to do the actual budgeting process.

You can set this up in many ways. I use two tools:

1. A calendar for seeing how money will "flow" through the month
2. A categorized budget to help me plan with the big picture in mind

Let's start with the Cash Flow Calendar.

For anyone just starting out in the budgeting process, I want you to use this tool exclusively (don't use the categorized budget to start) until you've gotten the complete hang of it and have done the budget with this tool at least a few months without any major hiccups. To complete the Cash Flow Calendar, fill in the days of the month on the worksheet, as appropriate (I use the smallest gray boxes in the upper left of each day). Second, using your completed Income Sources Worksheet, list the money you will receive throughout the month in the appropriate days (for instance, if you will receive $1,200 on the 15th and 30th of the month, put "+1,200" on each of those dates). Third, using your completed Irregular Bills and Monthly Bills Worksheets, list the money you will pay out throughout the month in the appropriate days (for instance, if you have a $75 electric bill due on the 20th of the month, put "-75" on that date). When it comes to things such as gas and food, you will need to plan when and how often you will make those purchases during the month and put the appropriate amounts on your selected dates. Once you've entered everything from your three worksheets onto the calendar (thus capturing all your income and expenses for the month), you are done! The purpose of the calendar is threefold:

1. I've not yet worked with anyone responsible for caring for his/her household finances who didn't know how to read and use a calendar. This familiarity helps you get over the fear of the unknown. A calendar is familiar, comfortable, easy.

2. If you begin at the first of the month and do the addition of your income and the subtraction of your expenses, you can see a fairly complete picture of whether or not you will have enough income to cover your expenses. This gives you the chance to adjust and prioritize your spending before the month begins and, if necessary, begin making arrangements with creditors and/or seeking out ways to earn additional income.

3. If unexpected expenses come up, or you have expenses too large for your income to cover, you won't be surprised because you can see ahead to know what's coming and plan accordingly.

If you'd like to compare your Cash Flow Calendar with an example, one is provided for you in the Appendix. Fair warning: It takes longer to complete a budget using a calendar than using the Categorized Budget method. A calendar, however, forces you to pay attention to how your money will "flow through the month." Additionally, if you are past due on any bills or must prioritize who you will pay each month due to a lack of funds in your overall budget, this method will give you a clearer picture of your situation. I highly recommend the Cash Flow Calendar method of budgeting for anyone who struggles to make ends meet each month and/or is regularly late on payments.

One final note based on a common question I get about the calendar: I ask you to list all your expenses based on their due date so you have an accurate picture of reality. Like a clock on the wall that tells you what time you must leave to avoid being late for work, listing your bills based on their due date shows you the date by which you must pay them to avoid them being late. You should avoid the habit of paying a bill on its due date every month simply because that's when it must be paid. If you have the money in hand and your budget says you can afford to pay the bill, pay the bill! Don't hold on to the money just because you have a few more days before it is due. This is asking for trouble. Wait until the last minute to pay a bill only if you aren't sure the income is going to be there to cover it and there is another more important expense (such as groceries).

Categorized Budget

The Categorized Budget is another way to approach setting up a monthly budget. Like the Cash Flow Calendar, it forces you to allocate your spending before the month begins and ensure you have a positive cash flow (in other words, it lets you know if there's enough money coming in to cover all your expenses). The major difference is that with a Categorized Budget, you are determining a "pool" of money for a given category and then must be disciplined enough to make that pool last for the entire month. My wife and I have been doing a budget since the day we got married and can now do our budget in about 10-15 minutes per month. We now use the Categorized Budget because we are comfortable with when our bills are due versus when our paychecks will come in and the Categorized Budget method is faster. But (and this is a big one), a Categorized Budget does not let you "see the money flow through the month" as a Cash Flow Calendar does. Thus, I recommend it only for those who know that (1) there is a positive cash flow and (2) the income from each paycheck can comfortably cover the expenses as they are due. If you need to do any prioritizing on bill payments and/or are past due on any bills, I recommend the Cash Flow Calendar.

In the Categorized Budget, you first need to select the major categories of your spending. I've given you a fairly complete example of a Categorized Budget in the Appendix. You should not expect to have all the same categories as the example, although you will have several of them. Second, determine which of your expenses from the Monthly Bills and Irregular Bills Worksheets goes into each category. As you add these up (per category) you should know how much you need to budget for that given category. Third, take your total monthly income and subtract the total amounts for each category. In the example, this is the AMOUNT column. The REMAINING column lists how much of your total month's income is left over after setting these aside. This will tell you whether you have enough money to cover the expenses for that month (positive cash flow). Make adjustments to the various categories and amounts until you are able to spend all the money on paper while covering all your necessary expenses. If you are unable to do this, you should consider using the Cash Flow Calendar and seek input from a competent financial counselor to help you with debt reduction and spending priorities.

The Envelope System

No matter which method of the monthly budget you use, I highly recommend that you make use of the envelope system for those pesky categories of your budget where you can't seem to behave with your money. The envelope system is very simple yet very powerful. Basically, the envelope system is this: For every category within your budget that you struggle with overspending, get an envelope and, on payday, place the appropriate budgeted amount in cash in the envelope. If you get paid once monthly, you'll put the total monthly amount in there. If you get paid twice monthly, you'll divide your monthly budgeted amount for that category in half and put that much in the envelope each payday. Each time you need to pay for an expense, pull out the cash in the envelope and pay for it! When the money is gone from the envelope, you're done until the next paycheck. You can never overspend using the envelope system because the money is gone. You can never leave the store with more stuff than allotted in your budget unless you want to risk a shoplifting conviction. The envelope system makes discipline with your budget category much easier because you simply spend whatever is in the envelope and when it is gone you know you are done.

My wife and I still use the envelope system for five major categories in our budget where we found ourselves overspending: gifts, entertainment, groceries, clothing, and miscellaneous household (this category includes supplies such as toilet paper, detergent, etc.). Although we could probably go back to using our check card or checks for these items, continuing to use cash keeps us from the temptation to overspend.

Since many people want to cheat or take shortcuts even with this simple method, let me give you a few helpful suggestions on using the envelope system. First, you need a different envelope for each category for which you decide to use cash. Don't just pick three or four categories, get cash for those categories, and then try to save a tree by putting all that cash in one envelope. You'll end up forgetting how much money you've spent in which category and how much is leftover, etc.. Please, for the love of your sanity, use one envelope for each category.

Second, let's say you walk into the grocery store with $400 in your envelope for the month's groceries and go a little overboard. The total when you check out at the register is $390. You walk out of the store with what you're sure are plenty of groceries to last the month, but then your teenage son walks up to you on the 20th of the month and asks why the fridge is empty. Ummmm…oops? You have $10 in your grocery budget, leaving $1 per day to make the rest of the month work for your family. Chances are, that isn't going to cut it. Ramen noodles are cheap, but this isn't college, and you shouldn't have put yourself and your family in that situation.

What's the solution? There may be several, but mine would be to commit to going grocery shopping once per week or once every two weeks, and then divide the cash the same way. Walk into the store not with your entire $400 but with the exact amount to cover the week or two weeks' worth of groceries. Does that mean you'd have to take a calculator and maybe say no to a few purchases, even if they're on a good sale? Of course it does. Does it mean you'd have groceries all month long? Of course it does!

When Stacy and I were starting out, this meant that we committed to going grocery shopping every Monday with only the cash from our envelope to cover that week's grocery needs. We agreed to make $75 per week for groceries work, so Stacy would walk in with her calculator, coupons, list, and exactly $75 cash. If there were four Mondays in a month, we'd budget $300 for that month's grocery budget; if there were five Mondays we'd budget $375. This ensured we behaved with our grocery expenditures.

One last thing on the envelope system: security. As I've spoken at events and workshops, people have regularly questioned me on how I feel about carrying around that much cash. They ask if I feel unsafe or like I run a greater risk of being robbed. In short–no, I'm not worried carrying around a little cash. At most, Stacy and I will probably have $500-600 that comes out each month for the envelopes, and by the time we have knocked out a few days in our month from that cash withdrawal, that total drops quickly. So, for all the potential muggers out there reading this, if you succeed in robbing Stacy and/ or me at just the right time, you might get a few hundred bucks. Then again, if you time it wrong, you might as well have robbed the local homeless man. (Also be aware that I might have to take you out if you try to rob us. My suggestion: Move on to a family who doesn't enjoy their second amendment right to keep and bear arms.)

What if There is Leftover Money?

As you complete your budget, you may have spent every penny on paper, just like a rightly-prepared budget should. Remember our math formula of a budget?

INCOME - SAVINGS - EXPENSES = 0

If you did your budget and realized the math worked out to where you have some money left over once you pay your required monthly bills, you need to do something to make a plan for that money or it will disappear. Plan for it or you will "magically" lose that cash. This is a very common occurrence when I meet with families. They prove the math of their situation works and there is surplus income, but they still struggle to explain where the leftover money goes. Hard as they may try, they just can't tell me what happened.

This is a very important step for those families who are on a variable income (commissioned sales, hourly pay with periodic overtime, etc.). I mentioned earlier that we would discuss what to do with the extra income you get above and beyond your strict budgeted amount (the amount you are confident you can plan on). This is where we pick that back up.

The process is very simple, but let me outline it in some detail so you can get this right the very first month you do your budget. Take out a blank sheet of paper and divide it into three columns: PRIORITY, ITEM, and AMOUNT. I used to call this sheet a "kill list" because I thought it was a good explanation of what you'd be doing with the things on that list. I've learned, however, that a better description is a "financial wish list" because these are the things you wish to accomplish when the extra money allows. Whatever you call it, your goal is to use the list to make plans for that extra income that might come in. Take a few minutes of your time with that sheet of paper to make a list of goals for your household and the associated costs. You may want to refer back to your Monthly Bills Worksheet, especially the notes column. Why? Because your Monthly Bills Worksheet should list all your outstanding debts, and I hope some of the goals on your wish list are to knock these debts out early. I don't want you making minimum payments for the rest of your life–I want to make your debt go away completely. Freedom is the goal, and making bigger payments on your debts will save you lots of money and get you out of debt faster (I bet you didn't see that one coming!). Let's look at an example.

PRIORITY	ITEM	AMT
1	Build 1-paycheck emergency fund	$1,100
7	Pay off Visa	$1,355
9	Pay off Student Loan	$11,690
10	Put down new carpet upstairs	$3,800
4	New car tires	$400
8	Pay off car early	$5,800
11	Build full emergency fund	$10,000
12	Take family to Disney World	$5,000
6	Replace kitchen stove	$600
3	Pay off American Express	$580
2	Pay off medical bill 1	$360
5	Pay off medical bill 2	$1,100

One way to knock out these priorities is to put them in order based on the overall balance (smallest to largest). For debts, I think this is the smartest move. We'll talk in detail about how to get rid of your debts in an upcoming chapter, but let's discuss a little bit of that here. Dave Ramsey calls his method for knocking out debts the "debt snowball," where you list your debts from smallest to largest (based on the total balance due) and pay extra on only that smallest balance. When it is paid off, move on to the next one, rolling the minimum payment from the one you just paid off onto the next one along with any extra money you can add to it. Rinse and repeat until all your debts (minus the house) are paid off. All you nerds out there are already telling me that this plan makes no sense mathematically, and you're right. But haven't we already established that personal finance has very little to do with math? I don't know about you, but if I have ten or fifteen bad guys (debts) coming at me, I just want as many of them as possible to go away. I don't care how small they are–I just want to know they're not coming after me!

"Teach your kids how to handle money or they will grow up and live in your basement."
–Dave Ramsey

Unlike Ramsey's debt snowball approach, I don't just want you to consider your debts on this wish list. Expand your thinking a little to include other important priorities for your family. Maybe your car is on its last legs. Don't be unrealistic and expect the car will last until you are out of debt. That is just setting you up to be careless and have no money to buy another one. At the same time, don't be ridiculous. If you really want out of debt, you have to make it a priority. If you think a big fancy vacation is more important than becoming debt free, that's your choice because it's your money. As a financial counselor, I'd tell you that such a choice tells me you aren't serious about getting out of debt. I know you'd get mad at me for saying that, but that's why people hire me to offer my advice–I am willing to talk straight to you because you can't make me sleep in the dog house if we have a disagreement. By the way, I want you to take an awesome vacation. I want it to be a huge vacation–celebrating your freedom from debt. This means you'd have to put off that big vacation a few years, but wouldn't it be worth it? That's something to consider.

Notice that on this list, the priorities are just that–priorities. They aren't unrealistic goals like "buy a new Ferrari." If you're in debt and can't pay cash for a used Honda, chances are you shouldn't list the purchase of an exotic sports car as a priority for your household. Be reasonable, discuss and agree on these priorities with your spouse if you're married, and make a huge deal out of accomplishing any of the items you put on the list. Completing one of the items on your list is a celebration-worthy event!

Why Does This Whole Budget Thing Matter?

If you've kept up with the past several pages, you realize that personal finance is so much more about behavior than it is about money. You also realize that discipline and diligence are required to make personal finance work. You've learned that a budget is just a tool to assist you, and that you must decide to make it work and then get about the task of actually doing it.

While I could give you lots of reasons why a budget

is so important, I can sum them all up in one phrase: A budget matters because if you don't do it, you will never succeed with money.

It is a proven fact that you can never outspend your desires. The best you will ever do is meet all your needs, most of your wants, and some of your wishes. For that reason, there is no better place to start than with creating a budget and putting yourself in charge of your finances, and there's no better time to start than now.

Action Step:

You read about how to do a budget using the worksheets in the Appendix in the back of this book. If you haven't already done so, take some time now to really go through this chapter and those worksheets, filling out what may be your first attempt at a budget. Don't worry if you find it difficult–just get started!

Chapter 6:
Really Loving Your Spouse

This is likely one of the most important sections in this entire book. Every major statistic screams for engaged couples to avoid getting married because more than half of the people who say "I Do" don't make it as a married couple. And, yet thousands of people exchange vows each and every day, committing to have and to hold 'til death do them part…or until it gets really hard and they don't feel like dealing with it anymore. Even worse, most studies point out that the number one cause of divorce finds it root in money problems. So as you consider the importance of getting this money thing right in your marriage, there likely isn't a more critical thing to nail down with your spouse than your priorities with money.

If you're married, you're already nodding your head in agreement, but let me go a bit further. How many of you reading these words know already that you'll never succeed with your finances if you and your spouse don't agree? Trust me–I've counseled dozens of couples who were on the brink of disaster in their marriage and in their finances because they couldn't agree on their financial priorities. Even though I am a firm believer that, as the man, I am ultimately responsible for my family's well-being and ensuring our financial needs are met, I'm not stupid enough to think my dear wife Stacy doesn't bring valuable input into our financial decision-making. You cannot pawn off the responsibility of your household finances on one spouse and allow the other to be off the hook.

It is common practice among married couples to keep separate checking/savings accounts and then separate out the bills in some agreed-upon manner and operate the household finances that way. This is dangerous and, if I may be so bold as to say, stupid! When a wife has separate finances, she is telling me she doesn't trust her husband. When a husband keeps separate accounts, he is telling me he has something to hide from his wife. When a couple can't combine their accounts when they get married but are willing to have children with each other, they are telling me that they aren't convinced this thing is going to last. Why not get a prenuptial agreement? I really cannot comprehend how you can successfully operate your household finances if the two of you do not fully share the income provided by any/all sources.

We have been blessed that Stacy does not have to work outside the home. This means she has some income, but it is sporadic and, for now, a lot less than my income from my steady job. Does this mean that if she needs something, I'm supposed to "loan" her the money since I love her and want to help meet her needs? That is just dumb. God's plan that "the two shall become one" in marriage applies here. If you are keeping separate accounts, stop it—immediately. You need to start having some good fights about money (and then making up) until you can get whatever keeps you from sharing your money out in the open and dealt with.

Let's clarify the difference between a money problem and a marriage problem. If you come home and your wife is mad that you bought a fancy new watch, you have a marriage problem. If you come home and your husband is mad that you spent the day at the spa, you have a marriage problem. If you can't save up and eventually accomplish these financial goals in your household, you may have a money problem.

I don't have a problem with someone making an extravagant purchase, and if you were to come see me for coaching I would probably tell you that very little is off-limits for you to buy. You must have a right recognition of what you can afford, however, and more importantly you and your spouse must agree a purchase is a reasonable priority for your household. The key is this: You must discuss any big purchases and agree on them before you just go out and spend the money. If you can't agree on a financial decision, the decision must be that you do not proceed until you can come to some sort of agreement. That may sound harsh, but I've seen too many wives bitter over their husband's prized bass boat or fancy tools and too many husbands bitter over their wife's designer purses or shoes or jewelry.

> *"If you want different results next year,*
> *what are you willing to change about*
> *what you are doing now?"*
> –Dan Miller

Have you ever heard of someone going out and making a really expensive purchase to spite their spouse? "I'll teach him to lie around all Saturday while I work to clean up the house. I'll go have that $400 spa treatment I wanted that he didn't get for my birthday." Have you done this? Come on–be honest. What about someone purposefully not paying a bill just so the spouse will feel the pain? "I work like a dog to bring home money for us to have food on the table and she does this? She goes and wastes $400 that we don't even have!?! I'll teach her. I'll just 'forget' to pay her car payment this month and see how she likes it when the bank calls." Having worked six years in the credit card business, most of it focused on collections, I know for a fact that this happens all the time.

Money is not a weapon to be used for mastering or punishing someone whom you feel has misbehaved. Money is a tool to foster open communication, goal-setting, and showing love to your spouse. Used rightly, money is how you and your spouse can discuss what is important to you, what worries you, what ambitions you have, and what is keeping you from accomplishing your dreams. Since money is the catalyst to all these discussions, it is sad that most couples never discuss money until there is a problem, and then they are rarely discussions but instead huge arguments. While I'm all about a good money fight and encourage those I counsel to have them all the time, I want the fight to be about airing out troubles and challenges, frustrations and sufferings–all aimed toward the goal of doing better with money as a couple and learning more about each other in the process.

So how do you start this discussion instead of having a big fight? Don't make it about the money–make it about the dreams you can accomplish together. Look back at how you did in the past and consider what you should do differently to make things better. As author and career coach Dan Miller wrote in his book No More Dreaded Mondays, "If you want different results next year, what are you willing to change about what you are doing now?" It is a great exercise in marital love to talk about every single expense that went through your household last month. It is easy enough to do–if your bank offers online banking, print off all your expenses from last month and spend an hour or two just reviewing where the money went. Look at the expenses you didn't plan on and those that were different from what you expected. Openly discuss where the money went and what you wish you would have done differently. It will be an amazing journey of growth for you and your spouse in both the communication you share and the way you focus your intensity on your finances.

Nerds and Free Spirits

The big problem with trying to get married couples to agree about money is that there are usually two major personality types in your relationship. The familiar notion that opposites attract usually applies here. Having two opposing views on money in a relationship is actually a good thing if handled correctly. Let me prove it. If you both agree on everything about money and your agreement is that it is smart to buy lottery tickets with at least 50% of your income, saving the rest for your annual pilgrimage to Vegas, sure that your winnings will cover groceries and housing needs, this is a bad plan. You are destined to be broke because you agree on a stupid plan. On the flip side, if you both agree on everything about money and your agreement is that you should both work three jobs so you can save every penny for your kids' college and your retirement, never considering that to do so means your kids will no longer know who you are and you won't be able to retire because you'll be dead at 50, this plan is equally bad. While those examples may seem silly, they aren't too far from reality in many households. You can totally agree with your spouse on some really dumb things. You know it's true.

Ideally, you want two distinct personalities in your marital relationship when discussing the finances. Borrowing directly from Dave Ramsey (can you tell I'm a big fan yet?), these two personality types are "what he calls the nerds" and "the free spirits." The hardcore nerds love doing the budget and love everything about dealing with the accounting aspect of money. They are total geeks and probably own a pocket protector (even if they won't admit it). This is the category in which I fall, so please take the preceding sentence as a compliment–I do. I love numbers. I balance my checkbook a little too often and spend a little too much time playing with math formulas and other "important" information as I go over our finances. The nerd thinks two things when working on the finances:

1. How much do I have to spend?
2. How much more can I bring in?

You have to be careful with the nerds because they aren't very good at letting go of money. My sister claims it takes a crowbar to pry my wallet open. I've been referred to as "cheap," and I claim it as a badge of honor. So what if I'm cheap? Well…I (and every other bean counter) have to be careful here. My wife likes to wear nice clothes and have a nice home. I want functional, she wants pretty. See the problem? If I'm not careful, I can hurt her feelings because it doesn't compute in my brain that throw pillows are an important budgetary item. I have to slow down and realize that my love for my wife requires me to exercise restraint in being stingy or cheap when it comes to the things that are important to her and that we can reasonably afford.

On the other side, you have the open-minded, free-spirited people who just want to be surrounded by nice things and enjoy life. The hardcore free spirits are the people you see featured on HGTV® or in Southern Living® magazine. These people are usually well-kept, have nice houses and hobbies such as cloud watching, gardening, shopping, and anything else that involves looking at pretty things. These people hate doing the budget because all it does is restrain them from being creative or thinking about more important things...such as redecorating a bedroom. This person thinks two things when forced to work on the finances:

1. How much can I spend?
2. How many nicer things can I bring in?

Notice the similarity (and at the same time, the stark contrast) between the two schools of thought? The free spirits often struggle to make ends meet because they don't keep track of their money and don't strategize about money at all–they just spend it. The nerd has to show restraint to not be stingy, while the free spirit has to be willing to stop spending so the household doesn't go broke! The free spirit has to be careful to recognize that groceries, gas, and the mortgage must come before the latest offering from Prada®.

Can you see how these two opposing schools of thought can create some serious conflict? Think about it–someone who hates to spend and loves to track every penny can be (and often is) married to someone who just wants to "make it work" and have a good time along the way. I know I may be sounding a little harsh toward the free spirits because I'm a nerd, and that's the biggest challenge of all for those who have my personality type. To say "okay...but" is a big problem in the nerd's vocabulary. Nerds have to learn to lighten up. For your wife to want a new living room rug is not evil! For your husband to want a new set of golf clubs is not evil! The question is always: "Given our current financial state and our family priorities, can we afford this?" If the answer is "yes," go for it! If the answer is "no," nerds can help the free spirit out by using their superpowers and mapping out a plan to help accomplish the financial goal. This shows love that will earn you some serious brownie points.

When it comes to doing the budget, the nerds can't rule supreme and the free spirits don't get a pass. Whoever the nerd is in your household may be the best person to prepare the budget and play around with the numbers, but the free spirit must at least understand the budget, have a say in what gets spent where, and ultimately sign off on the numbers before any money gets spent. The budget is a crucial place for communicating with your spouse and closing the gap between the extreme tendencies of the nerd and the free spirit. The budget helps to build a bridge between the opposing views, helping the nerd to lighten up and the free spirit to show some restraint.

One helpful practice I've found is to provide some "fun money" for each spouse. I probably have made it sound thus far as though you must discuss every penny spent in your household and agree even on the toilet paper that gets bought. That is a little overboard. When doing your budget, why not agree on an amount each month for his and her "fun money"? This is money that can be spent on anything. Get this amount out of the bank in cash on payday and then it is up to the husband to do whatever he wants with "his" money and up to the wife to do whatever she wants with "her" money. This is a little different from the concept of his money and her money we discussed earlier. This is just a set amount you agree upon as a part of your budget that allows each of you the freedom to go have a little fun.

Relating with money all comes down to sharing your heart with your spouse. Show him/her what is important to you, help him/her understand why it is important, and then listen to the response. While money is at the core of your discussion, it is not the focus–love and priorities are the two major focal points. In other words, you are working together to set the appropriate balance and boundaries for your household finances.

Action Steps:

Set up a date night for you and your spouse. The only topic of discussion: dreaming about what's important to the other person and to you as a couple. Share openly, passionately, and at length about what you dream about, and encourage your spouse to do the same. Make a big to-do out of it, and there are only two rules: NO FIGHTING ALLOWED and NO POO-POOING YOUR SPOUSE'S DREAMS.

Chapter 7:
Insurance:
The Bare Minimums

I hesitated to write this chapter, only because there are such differing opinions on the topic of what insurances you need and which are a waste of your money. Then I realized this is my book and therefore my opinion trumps all that stuff! You can disagree with me if you want and send me hate mail, but at least you read it and took a stand, and that means you had to consider the information and make some progress toward forming your own opinions about what insurance you really need. If I've gotten you that far, then we've hit some success. So I want to talk about the three types of insurance that I believe are critical to your financial plan based on what I've witnessed and learned through the counseling I've done over the years. One type of insurance I did not include is auto insurance because the law requires this type of insurance in most states and there are far fewer ways you can be swindled with car insurance than with the three I will discuss.

Life Insurance

You are going to die. That wasn't a threat. Unless the world ends first, you will die one day. When you die, you will probably leave at least one or two people behind who will wonder where you went and may even be sad about your passing. The hope is that there will be many more than that and your passing will have an impact on lots of people. Likely, your passing will have a huge financial impact on your immediate family. From the expense of a funeral and burial (roughly $10,000 based on national averages) all the way to the replacement of daily income, someone is probably going to have to make some financial changes because you are no longer there. Thus, life insurance is very important, especially for those of you without a lot of savings. Let me explain.

I wholeheartedly believe that the sole purpose of a life insurance policy is to replace the income of someone who dies so the people left behind don't become destitute. If I died tomorrow and had no insurance, Stacy and our kids would have very little steady income and no health insurance. That's a scary thought. She would have to rely on our savings for a while, then figure out a way to get a job and child care for the kids, all while mourning my loss (at least I hope she'd be mourning!). My death could easily cause a massive financial shock wave. But it wouldn't because I have a nice level-term life insurance policy that should take care of them if I die. So while she would probably mourn, she should never have to worry about finances. I have a policy on myself because I provide the primary source of our household income.

For how long do I need to make sure we have an insurance policy covering me? For as long as we need my income. As we progress in our financial goals to where we become less and less dependent on my paycheck, we also become less and less dependent on a life insurance policy covering me.

I know what you want to ask–"how much insurance do I need?" Clearly understanding the purpose of that life insurance policy helps us answer this question. Like your emergency fund, life insurance is protection against losing everything because of a major unexpected expense or major change in your overall financial well-being. Death of the primary breadwinner definitely qualifies here. So you need enough insurance to allow the interest income to be sufficient to provide an amount at least equal to your salary. The goal is for those you leave behind to be able to invest the lump sum of the insurance payout and live off the interest. To make this possible, most financial counselors teach (and I agree) that you should get a policy valued at ten times the amount of income you need to replace.

For example, if you make $50,000 per year, get at least a $500,000 policy. Since the goal is to be able to replace your income by living off the interest, that means you'd be investing in something that would need to earn roughly 10% per year (10% of $500,000 is $50,000; if you're earning 10% per year, your family could withdraw $50,000 off the $500,000 policy payout and never touch the principal and repeat that process each year indefinitely). I understand that oversimplifies the process a bit because there will be years where you'll earn less than 10% and years you'll earn more. Don't miss the point–if you have a large lump sum of money that is well invested, you can expect a reasonable amount of interest income that you can draw off the top each time there is a decent gain and use it for living expenses.

Now your next question is probably–"what kind of life insurance should I get?" There are literally thousands of options out there for life insurance. They can really be boiled down into two major categories: "term" and "permanent." Term insurance is, as it sounds, insurance that is provided only for a given term, and the insurance coverage ends when that term is over. Permanent insurance provides coverage for as long as you keep paying premiums, up until you die or are disqualified for coverage based on some life event. Permanent insurances are often referred to as "whole life" or "universal life" policies, and these have dozens of variations and many other less-frequently-used names. If you don't see the word "term" in the name of the product, it is very likely "permanent" insurance of some sort.

With term policies, all your costs and coverages are set up front. For example, if you request a 20-year, $500,000 level-term policy and, based on your age and health, are quoted that policy at $350 per year, you will pay $350 per year every year for 20 years. At the end of the 20 years, the insurance coverage ends and you both walk away. The longer the coverage term, the poorer your health, and/or the higher your age, the more the insurance costs (because if you are sick and as you get older, the risk of your dying goes up–bet you didn't see that one coming).

Term insurance is hands-down the cheapest form of life insurance. I recommend level-term insurance because it is affordable, it isn't fancy (because it doesn't need to be), and it acts just as it should–as insurance and nothing more. Seek a term that is long enough to cover the time for which you expect to be working to provide income for someone who will depend on that paycheck if you were to die. For example, if you are doing great with your investments and plan to retire at age 50, get a term sufficient to insure you at least until you're 50 (at a bare minimum). If you have very little saved and thus will need to work from now until you are at least 65, get a policy that will cover you for the longer period. Keep in mind that the longer the term (especially as you get above age 60), the higher the cost of the coverage.

Permanent policies are often advertised as life insurance plans that offer a built-in investment plan. They proclaim that term life insurance only gives you insurance and when that coverage is over you will, in effect, have paid to receive no benefit. They also proclaim that with their plan, you can invest and save for later while at the same time having insurance coverage. Without going into a lot of details, let me first say that these claims are true. Let me also say, however, that this moves the insurance plan out of its primary purpose and makes you pay (and almost always pay too much) for an added component. I suggest that you do not complicate your insurance purchases at all and don't pay extra for insurance just because it may have some built-in savings plan. While there may be one out there somewhere, I have never been able to locate a whole life or universal life plan that costs less or provided as good a level of coverage as a level-term plan. I'll take my investing somewhere else and let my insurance function as insurance.

One last point about insurance. Instead of arguing the merits of term vs. permanent policies: Go get a quote. Call up your insurance agent and tell him you'd like a quote on a life insurance policy that is ten times your annual income and then let the numbers decide which type of policy you purchase. Don't get sold on any hype– remember the purpose of life insurance (to replace your income if you die so your family won't be destitute) and only pay for what you need. But whatever you do, don't skip this coverage. Your family is counting on you.

Health Insurance

Like life insurance, people have hugely varied opinions about whether or not you need health insurance and, if you do need it, how much you really need. Since this chapter is all about the bare minimums of insurance, I'll start by saying that I land in the camp that believes you should never be without some form of health insurance. The number one cause of personal bankruptcy in America is medical debt. You don't plan on having a heart attack or being diagnosed with cancer, but you certainly want good medical treatment if it happens to you.

You've read enough of this book thus far to know I've not worried about making you mad, so let me make my first (maybe my only) political statement in this book:–I believe it is exclusively because our country can't get a grip on balancing medical needs with associated costs that we are in much of the financial mess we are in. Let me explain. If I walk into the doctor's office for a routine visit, he is going to bill my insurance company something for that appointment (as well as any payment I provide him). He bills them an amount (almost always) much higher than what he would charge if I walked in and said I just want to pay cash for the whole thing and be done with it. Why does he charge them more? Because the system is so messed up that he has to cover his costs for the paperwork; and some of the claims that get denied. He also has to accept some patients who can't afford to pay him; etc., etc.

Billing and ultimately receiving payment is a huge, complicated, messy, and confusing affair for your doctor. This explains, in part, why many doctors restrict the insurance plans they accept and why some don't accept insurance at all, despite the legal requirements in place and government intervention.

Despite all the problems with our insurance system, I do believe it is a necessary evil because you probably aren't prepared to pay $1,000,000+ (yes, those six zeros indicate million) in medical bills. If you get cancer and go through treatments, that bill may very well be a million dollars or more by the time it is all said and done. I am a big proponent of keeping you out of bankruptcy, and so insurance is almost always worth every penny you pay for reasonable coverage. Notice also I said reasonable coverage. I wish I could give you the exact formula for which insurance plan is perfect for you, but it truly depends on your personal medical needs and your willingness to take on some of the risk of having to pay your own medical expenses if/when something goes wrong.

Some insurance plans cover every doctor's visit, every prescription, and every other conceivable treatment out there (acupuncture, chiropractic, massage therapy, gym membership, etc.). If you want to pay for that type of luxury plan, be my guest. I don't believe you need this much insurance, though, and I believe you can do much better for yourself and your family if you step down on what gets covered and when coverage kicks in. If you are paying for your own insurance, you know every dollar counts, so what should you be looking for? Remember, we're looking at minimums:

- *Major medical coverage*–if you are in an accident or have a major illness and require hospitalization, you want to be sure you don't have to pay that entire bill.
- *A deductible that will kick in before your emergency fund is stretched too far*–ideally, you should have an emergency fund of several months' worth of expenses. Let's assume $10,000 is in your account for your emergency fund. In this case, you could get a policy that had a $5,000 annual deductible and be in great shape (and save lots of money over a traditional policy).
- *An out-of-pocket maximum that won't break you*– similar to having a higher deductible, if you're willing to risk a bit higher out-of-pocket maximum (the maximum amount you will have to spend before your insurance takes over paying for 100% of the medical expenses for that year), you can save lots of money.

Assuming the same $10,000 emergency fund with a policy that has a $5,000 deductible, you may seek out having something like a $7,000 maximum out of pocket. This still leaves you $3,000 worth of emergency fund money to live on while this medical issue is being dealt with. That isn't much, but it is something.

- *No annual or lifetime caps on coverage*–some policies will end their coverage after a certain amount of bills are paid. Usually the number is pretty high, such as $5,000,000, but I've seen many instances where $5,000,000 didn't cover the medical expenses from a major medical event or series of events. Look for a policy that doesn't cap its coverage. Due to the Affordable Care Act (ACA), at the time of this writing insurers cannot place an annual or lifetime limit except on non-essential health benefits. There are also clauses that allow existing policies to be grandfathered in. In other words, despite the ACA, you still need to watch out for this one.

It is nice to have prescription drug coverage, wellness exam coverage, and maternity benefits, but most people do not require these and can handle these expenses as they arise. The one major exception would be someone who is already taking many medications. Some prescription drugs are extremely expensive; if you can find a policy that covers prescriptions without a great deal of extra cost, I'd recommend you get that feature as well.

There is another option if traditional health insurance is not available to you or the cost is prohibitively high–healthcare sharing. If you do not have insurance coverage available from an employer, health care sharing programs are often excellent alternatives and generally meet the guidelines I outlined above.

While several such programs are out there, two I have researched and would recommend are: Medi-Share (*https://mychristiancare.org/medi-share/*) and Samaritan Ministries (*http://samaritanministries.org/*). Both of these organizations are faith-based and work on the principle that you pay in a monthly "share" that goes to meet others' needs. If you have a medical need, other members assist you.

There are thousands of stories of people who didn't have insurance and it sunk their financial ship. There are also thousands of stories of people who had too little insurance and met the same demise. Don't be under-insured. At least meet these bare minimums to cover whatever medical issue may arise.

Long-Term Disability Insurance

Many employers offer short-term disability insurance. This covers you by providing at least a percentage of your lost salary if you suffer an injury or serious illness that prevents you from going to work for more than a few days. With most policies, coverage kicks in when you have used up all your sick leave, and often your vacation or any other discretionary time. The percentage of your overall salary that is provided with short-term disability varies, but is usually ultimately reduced to about 50-60% of your salary. Short-term disability usually lasts no more than six months before coverage ends and you either have no coverage or move into long-term disability.

Long-term disability coverage (like the other insurances we've discussed) is designed to keep you from going bankrupt because of an unexpected illness or injury that keeps you from going back to work. It behaves much like short-term disability insurance in that it pays you a percentage of the salary you would have made if you were working, except it pays that amount for a longer period of time. You can get 5-year, 10-year, and even "until age 65" coverage with long-term disability.

My advice is to get long-term disability coverage that has a long elimination period (the amount of time you're out of work until the coverage kicks in) and that has the longest benefit period you can afford. A good policy would be one that has a one-year elimination period and coverage until age 65. This would mean you'd need to live off savings for a year, and then you'd be covered until age 65. This is a good policy if you have an emergency fund (are you seeing the trend here yet? Get a big emergency fund once you're out of debt) and it will not be too expensive because the insurance company knows you have to be out of work for at least a year before it will cost them anything to cover you.

Keep in mind that, whether or not you have short-term disability coverage, you will need to be ready to rely on your emergency fund if you're injured and can't work for a while. Many employers offer this type of short-term coverage (as I mentioned), but many do not. Either way, you should not expect to receive 100% of your salary if you are unable to work–this is just common sense. Thus, I want to end this chapter by emphasizing (again) the critical importance of having an emergency fund that will allow you to continue putting food on the table, a roof over your head, and lights on in your home in case something keeps you from bringing in an income for a period of time. Do not be lazy with this financial goal!

Action Steps/Questions:

1. Based on what you read here, are you over- or under-insured?

2. Why do you have the insurance coverage you have now?

3. Call your insurance agent or go online to a reputable company such as *http://www.zanderinsurance.com* and get quotes on any insurance I mentioned in this chapter. If traditional health insurance isn't available or affordable for you, check out Medi-Share and Samaritan Ministries to see if they are worthwhile options.

Action Steps/Questions:

1. Based on what you read here, are you over- or under-insured?

2. Why do you have the insurance coverage you have now?

3. Call your insurance agent or go online to a reputable company such as *http://www.zanderinsurance.com* and get quotes on any insurance I mentioned in this chapter. If traditional health insurance isn't available or affordable for you, check out Medi-Share and Samaritan Ministries to see if they are worthwhile options.

65

Chapter 8:
Tackling Debt

I know we've talked about several topics thus far that have sung the praises of having a big emergency fund and lots of savings, but you don't want to get there too quickly. My overall approach to financial fitness can be summed up by Romans 13:8, which says we should "let no debt remain outstanding, except the continuing debt to love one another, for he who loves his fellowman has fulfilled the law" (NIV). I don't want you to have debt. I don't want you to owe for your house, your car(s), your education, your vacation, your clothes, your medicine–I don't want you to have any debt. Clear enough? The obvious question is to figure out how to get out of debt and stay out of it for good. Now that I have (I hope) laid a solid foundation for living on less than you make, doing a budget every month that includes savings as a priority, and making sure you and your spouse are on the same page, getting out of debt can flow naturally from accomplishing those goals. So what are the steps for getting out of debt? I offer five simple steps that will help you get out of debt as quickly as possible and without any tricks, gimmicks, or dangerous risks along the way. We'll get into those shortly.

Remember, It Isn't About Math

In most households, there is more than sufficient income to cover the required expenses of that household. Somehow, the math works, but the budget doesn't. As you've learned in the preceding pages, very little of personal finance has to do with math. If you can add, subtract, multiply, and divide, you've got more than sufficient math skills to handle the math involved in doing your household finances. So what's the problem? You are. You like buying stuff and you don't like dealing with paperwork, so you get lazy when it comes to managing your finances.

I'll admit there are plenty of households that struggle to make ends meet because there really is a math problem, but that is usually an easier fix than for those who just don't manage the money well. For those with a math problem, finding a better job or a temporary second job or cutting unnecessary expenses can be the solution. It is not hard to fix the math problem in most cases.

What we have to fix for the majority of cases is the behavior problem. In the "Looking Back to See the Significance" section, I outlined that it is your behavior that decides whether or not you will succeed with your finances, and I reiterate that here because there are lots of supposed shortcuts to getting out of debt, cleaning up your credit score and avoiding paying back the money you owe. Don't be foolish–you got into the mess, so have the discipline and maturity to work your way out of it. What behaviors got you into the mess? Those are the behaviors that have to change.

Interest Calculations: the Math

Even though I just told you a bunch of reasons personal finance has nothing to do with math, that doesn't mean I want you to be ignorant of how the math works. I don't want it to be your focus, but I definitely want you to be able to understand how the numbers work so you can make educated decisions for yourself and apply this understanding to help others who may be struggling. Plus, what kind of self-proclaiming nerd would I be if I didn't have some math in this book!?

First, let's make sure we're all on the same page about what interest actually is. Interest is the amount you agree to pay (usually as a percentage of the amount borrowed) in addition to the amount you borrow (known as the principal balance). You will often see this advertised as __% APR (annual percentage rate). For example, if you borrow $1,000 at 10% APR, you will be paying 10% interest (or $100) each year until the principal balance is 0. As the principal balance goes down, you will pay less in interest. This is because you are paying 10% per year. So, if you pay $500 of that $1,000 off in the first year, the next year you'll only be paying $50 in interest (10% of the remaining principal balance, $500). This is a very simplified approach to interest and repayment terms, but it should give you a general idea of how it works.

Many people ask me why creditors charge interest or why the interest rates are so high. There are several answers to this question. Let's look at a few of them by way of a simple example. Let's assume you have $1,000 in hand. With that $1,000 you could go to the bank and, without risk, deposit it in a savings account and earn a small amount of interest (maybe 0.1-0.3%). You could deposit that same $1,000 in a money market account, taking a small risk, and earn a bit better interest (maybe 1-1.5%). You could take that same $1,000 and play the slots in Las Vegas and possibly earn a lot. Your risk in Las Vegas, though, is very high.

Basically, interest (and interest rates) work the same way. Interest is a measure of risk. If you have excellent credit, you should expect to pay a low amount of interest. Because the creditor isn't taking much risk, he shouldn't expect to get much return. On the flip side, if you have very poor credit, you should expect to pay a high amount of interest, especially on unsecured debt. The creditor is taking a much higher risk of losing the money based on your past performance and so he expects a much higher return on his money.

Before we move on, let's look at a few examples. Notice that the math is the same and the general approach is the same.

Example 1: Let's assume you have a credit card with a $3,500 balance and your current APR is 21%. For simplicity, we'll assume interest compounds monthly. How much should the interest portion of your payment be for this month?

First, let's calculate the monthly interest rate:

21% APR ÷ 12 months = 1.75% monthly rate

Next, let's multiply that by the current balance:

$3,500 balance x 1.75% monthly rate = $61.25 in interest

As you can see from the example above, just by having a $3,500 credit card balance, you have to pay $61.25 every month in interest alone! No wonder it takes you forever to pay off credit card balances if you pay only minimum payments.

Example 2: Let's assume you have a mortgage with a $120,000 balance and your current APR is 6%. For simplicity, we'll assume interest compounds monthly. How much should the interest portion of your payment be for this month?

First, let's calculate the monthly interest rate:

6% APR ÷ 12 months = 0.5% monthly rate

Next, let's multiply that by the current balance:

$120,000 balance x 0.5% monthly rate = $600.00 in interest

As you can see from this example of a mortgage, you end up paying $600.00 in interest before any of the $120,000 principal balance is touched. This makes it seem like it might be good to be in the lending business if you have some money.

Looking at these examples, you should be able to take out virtually any of your bills and do the math. Figure out the monthly interest rate, multiply that amount by last month's ending balance, and you should come up with a number close to the number your bill shows as the interest amount for this month. The difference in numbers likely comes from the way the interest is calculated. Companies may use a daily compounding rate (APR ÷ 365), a monthly compounding rate (like our examples, APR ÷ 12) or a true annual compounding rate (APR) depending on the type of loan and the general repayment terms. This will make the numbers vary slightly. Hint: The daily compounding works most to the lender's advantage, so most lenders use this method.

The Five Steps

Now that you have a basic understanding of the math involved in getting out of debt, let's dive into the five steps I teach to get you out of debt...permanently.

1. Cut Expenses
2. Maximize Income
3. Get current on everything*
4. Use Dave Ramsey's debt snowball method to arrange your debts
5. Make a call every time you're ready to pay something off

Step 1: Cut Expenses

For the time that you are working to become debt free, say "no" to a lot of those unnecessary expenses in your life. For Stacy and me, this meant looking at things such as cable or super-fancy vacations and agreeing they could wait. Instead, we signed up for Netflix and went camping or on brief road trips to visit out-of-town family. Cut out every expense that isn't necessary for the sanity of your household. Now don't get mad at me–I don't want you to stop having fun. I just want you to remember that you are on a mission, and when the mission is accomplished you are ready to (and I expect you to) have a big celebration! In the meantime, you shouldn't be spending any money unnecessarily while you're focusing on getting out of debt.

As a part of this process, you should review every bill for which you owe any amount. Look at the overall balance, the interest rate, the minimum payment amount, the due dates, and be sure you understand the general terms so you can know how to use them to your advantage. Make a note of any bills that have an exceptionally high interest rate (for example, with credit cards, this would be anything over 12% APR). Also make note of any that are past due. This will become very important in Step 3 and will help you have a better understanding of what battles you should fight in your war against debt.

Step 2: Maximize Income

Just like you'll be saying "no" to a lot of the extra expenses in your household, you should also consider saying "yes" to a lot of the opportunities to earn some extra income. Explore your entrepreneurial side. When our mortgage balance was down to $20,000 and Stacy and I set a goal to pay off our house within the next 12 months, we both did a myriad of things to earn some extra cash. What can you do that people are willing to pay you to do? Keep it legal and keep it simple, but say "yes" to as many decent opportunities to make some extra money as you can to be able to throw extra money toward paying off your debts.

Before you go out and get three extra jobs and only get to sleep three hours each night because of this advice, let me calm you down a bit. You can overextend your time if you're not careful. Don't take just anything that comes along that will earn you a few dollars. If you are going to have to spend hours and hours of your time to earn just a small amount of money, recognize that your family would likely prefer you over than those few extra dollars paid toward debts. Don't make this a quest to see how many hours you can work. Keep some balance and remember that your family is much more important than any job.

Step 3: Get Current on Everything*

If you are committed to getting out of debt, the very first thing you must do is stop getting deeper in debt! This is such an obvious statement (I hope) that you are nodding your head, thinking, "Barry, I knew that without having to read this book." Good! Your first real step toward becoming debt free is to stop paying late fees and other things that result from being past due on your bills. If you're paying $25 per month on a credit card bill and paying it even one day late, you're being charged a $25-$35 late fee so you are potentially losing $10 per month if you consistently pay late. Poor people and lazy people pay late fees and foolish "gotchas" every month. Don't go there. Get every bill up to date and in good standing so you can avoid all those fees.

If you're behind on a lot of bills, I know this step may take some time. Just as it took you some time to get past due, it will take even longer to get back up to date. Don't act desperately. Just buckle down, cut expenses to the bone, and do everything (legal) you can do to bring in extra income until you're up to date on your bills. Even though this short-term sacrifice may be hard, it will save you a ton of heartache, aggravation, and more cash than you can imagine.

There is one exception to my rule of bringing every bill up to date in this step (hence the asterisk * on this step). If you have an extremely old debt that is currently lying around dormant somewhere at a collection agency, don't touch that one...for now. I only want you to make sure all your bills that come in and are requesting payment are up to date. Those that you've let go for a while can sit there a while longer. You should ultimately pay back all your debts (see Psalm 37:21) and should make every effort to do so. You do not, however, want to bring more trouble on an already difficult situation by dealing with those creditors who have, for the time being, stopped trying to collect. If/when they contact you about the debt and ask for payment and/or when you've gotten better control over your situation, then you should move on to your dormant debts.

There is one last thing about this step that you should be aware of–the concept of time-barred debt. Since every state has different laws about what constitutes a time-barred debt and exactly how it works, let me simply introduce you to the term and give you a very brief overview of what it is. Time-barred debt is debt that is too old for a collector to take legal action if you do not pay. If you have some debts that are at least three years old (meaning it has been at least three years since you have made a payment), do a quick online search on this term "time-barred debt" and you will find a wealth of information. More specifically, you should determine your state's laws about what constitutes a time-barred debt and how you should proceed. To find your state's laws about time-barred debt, visit the website of your state's Attorney General.

> *"The wicked borrow and do not repay, but the*
> *righteous give generously."*
> –Psalm 37:21 (NIV)

Step 4: Use Dave Ramsey's Debt Snowball Method

Since I want to appropriately give credit for this method to Dave Ramsey, I'll provide the explanation for this method directly from Dave's website[1] and let him explain how it works:

> *In the debt snowball, you list your debts*
> *smallest to largest by amount owed. Don't*
> *worry about interest rates. We don't care if*
> *one debt has a 2% rate and another one has*

---

1   *http://www.daveramsey.com/article/debt-snowball-breakdown/lifeandmoney_debt/*

a 22% rate. If you'd done the math properly, you wouldn't have gone into credit card debt in the first place. List the debts smallest to largest.

Now it's time to make progress. Pay minimum payments on all of the debts except the smallest one, and attack that with a vengeance. We're talking gazelle intense, sell-out, get-this-thing-out-of-my-life-forever energy. Once it's gone, take the money you were putting toward that debt, plus any extra money you find, and attack the next debt on the list. Once it's gone, take that combined payment and go to the next debt. Knock them out one by one.

Here's an example. Let's say you have the following debts:

- $500 medical bill (payment of $50 a month)
- $2,500 credit card debt ($63 payment)
- $7,000 car loan ($135 payment)
- $10,000 student loan ($96 payment)

In the debt snowball, we would list the debts in that order (remember, ignore the interest rates). Start by making the minimum payments on everything but the medical bill. For this example, let's say you find an extra $500 each month to go toward that debt by getting an extra job, slashing your lifestyle to nothing, and going crazy. That's very doable.

Since you are paying $550 a month on the medical bill (the $50 payment plus the $500 extra), that medical bill won't even last a *month. Now, take that $550 and attack the credit card debt. When that happens, you'll be paying $613 on the plastic (the freed up $550 plus the $63 minimum payment). In about four months, wave bye-bye to the credit card. You've paid it off!*

Now we're at the car debt. Punch that car note in the face to the tune of $748 a month (the freed-up $613 plus the $135 monthly payment). In 10 months, it will drive off into the sunset. Now you're on fire!

Once you've gotten to the student loan, you will be putting $844 a month on it. It will only last about 12 months. After that, Sallie Mae better get used to living somewhere else, because you've kicked her out!

Because of hard work and sacrifice, you have paid off $20,000 in debt in only 27 months using the debt snowball! Congratulations!

The point of the debt snowball is behavior modification. In our example, if you start paying on the student loan first because it's the largest debt, you won't see it leave for a while. You'll see numbers going down on a page, but that's it. Pretty soon, you'll lose steam and stop paying extra, but you'll still have all your debts hanging around.

But when you ditch the small debt first, you see progress. That one debt is out of your life forever. Soon the second debt will follow, and then the next. When you see that the plan is working, you'll stick to it. By sticking to it, you'll eventually succeed in becoming debt-free!

I couldn't have explained it any better myself, so I didn't even try.. I've counseled dozens of people on how to pay off their debts using this simple method and have found no method simpler or better. Remember, however, that I do ask you to be conscious of other priorities in your life. As I outlined in the "What if There is Leftover Money?" section, I don't want you to ignore danger signs of pending financial crisis like a car that just turned over 300,000 miles or a pink slip in your box at work. If you have a major consideration like this on the horizon, pause the debt snowball or at least include your upcoming financial need in your priority list as you are working through the debt snowball.

Step 5: Make a Phone Call Every Time You're Ready to Pay Something Off

This is something you won't read in many books on getting out of debt or hear in many discussions on the topic. Why? I'm not really sure. I've always been a fan of getting the best deal possible, so why shouldn't you do it with your debt? Whenever you are close to being ready to pay off a debt, you should pull out the bill, find the number for the company, and call them. What is the point of the call? To ask for a discount. Simply tell them you have some cash in hand and want to pay off this debt, but want a discount for paying in full. In my experience you'll get a discount about 60% of the time. Worst case, you spent a few minutes and still get to pay them off.

A word of caution—we're not looking for a settlement in most cases. A settlement, by definition, is when your creditor forgives a percentage of the debt as a method of getting you to pay (usually when you're past due). A settlement can impact your credit score negatively and have tax implications. I won't get into the details of a credit settlement here, but I will tell you that, unless you are in trouble with collections, this isn't what you are after. I'm asking you instead to call and ask them if they'll waive a month or two worth of interest charges or (if you've been past due) some late fees. If you've got a $1,500 balance on your credit card at a 29% interest rate, having them waive even one month of interest can amount to a $37 savings. This may not sound significant, but if I paid you $37 for every 15-minute phone call you could make in a regular workday, how long would you take for lunch?

Make this call only when you are ready to pay the debt off completely, or are at least very close to having the full amount. If you have a $400 balance on a debt and only $300 in hand, call and ask if they'll waive $100 worth of interest/fees if you pay it in full. The worst they'll say is no. If they say yes, be sure to ask for confirmation of that waived amount either via email or letter. Don't give them your payment information by phone because that can cause all kinds of problems. But do ask–I've seen people save hundreds of dollars simply by asking for a discount.

Summary

So there you have it. I can't tell you how quickly you'll get out of debt if you follow these steps, but if you sit down and do the math, I can tell you it will probably be faster than your math tells you. Why? Because once you get started, you'll build momentum and learn how to focus your energy! Don't make it complicated, don't make it hard, and don't wait to get started.

Action Steps/Questions

1. Review your list of all your bills. Are you paying more than you should on any of them? If so, call the company and reduce the monthly expense or eliminate it altogether.

2. Are you withholding too much in payroll taxes so you can have a big refund? Do you have unnecessary insurance coverage that comes out of your paycheck? Do you have hobbies someone will pay you to do? Make a list of five ways you can generate some extra income to get out of debt.

---

3. Be sure you are not past due on any bills. If you are, make getting them current a big priority and throw any extra income possible toward bringing those bills up to date.

Chapter 9:
Act Like a Millionaire

"It is easier to believe a lie that one has heard a thousand times than to believe a fact that one has never heard before."
–Robert S. Lynd

Getting out of debt is hard work because you have to commit yourself to doing it and then have the discipline to stick with it. It is not, however, a difficult process. The five steps are really very simple and done with even a little care, will result in your freedom from debt. So what's next? Why not try living like a millionaire? Thomas Stanley wrote an excellent book titled *The Millionaire Next Door*. He studied the "average" millionaire and looked for the success factors that brought them into such wealth. I highly recommend the book, and I highly recommend that you learn to live like the people in the book. Three of the success factors from his findings are how you can immediately begin living like a millionaire and start working your way to becoming one:

Success Factor 1:
Spend less than you earn.

If you are always spending up to or above what you earn, you will never increase your net worth, no matter how much you earn. Look at every source of income and every expense flowing through your household and make sure you are consistently spending less than you earn. Then make adjustments to improve the ratio of income to expenses. As simple as this tip may sound, I am consistently shocked at how often people spend every penny they bring in. It is not rare to find people who consistently spend more than they bring in while holding the attitude that they'll eventually make it work. Don't outspend your income.

Success Factor 2: Avoid buying status objects or leading a status lifestyle.

Buying expensive status objects such as a new luxury car or branded consumer goods places you in a cycle of trying to compete with "the Joneses" and makes it more difficult to make reasonable financial choices. There is an old Lending Tree® commercial that sums it up well. In it, the guy is talking about how he has a great family, a huge house in a nice neighborhood, a new car, a golf club membership, etc., etc. He then rhetorically asks the camera, "How do I do it?" His response is what is so powerful. He says, "I'm in debt up to my eyeballs...I can barely pay my finance charges...somebody help me." You should check this commercial out on YouTube. Don't be this guy. Look at the Joneses from a distance and recognize they have great stuff... that they'll be paying for the rest of their lives. Study how the Joneses live and what they drive, study who they are around, and then, most importantly, study how happy they really are. You'll often find there isn't much beyond the stuff.

Success Factor 3:
Take financial risks only
when they are worth the reward.

There are all kinds of supposed shortcuts to financial freedom. You see them on TV, hear about them on the radio, and yet somehow they sound too good to be true. Simply put, they are. There is no substitute for hard work. You can't take any shortcuts in becoming debt free. While the focus of this book isn't about investing and neither is Dr. Stanley's, let's explore this idea using investing as a frame of reference. People regularly ask me my opinion on where to invest their money. When I ask them whether or not they have any debt, most tell me they do. My advice for anyone who is in any sort of debt (except your house) is to "invest" in becoming debt free. With the ups and downs of the stock market and the unknown future of your job, your health, and countless other uncertainties, getting out of debt is the primary financial risk I recommend you take.

Why is getting out of debt a financial risk? Because by not putting your money into some sort of investment and instead paying down your debts, you're missing out on the opportunity to make money if the market does well. This is a tough pill to swallow for many folks, but I'm willing to take that risk until there is no debt (except a reasonable mortgage) in the picture. Think about it. If you're paying off a credit card that has been costing you 29% interest, you are not paying 29% interest when that debt is gone. That's pretty close to the same thing as earning 29% on your money. That's a good return in any market!

Let's also look at two scenarios:

Scenario 1:

You have a good-paying job that pays enough to cover all your minimum payments on about $40,000 worth of debt (credit cards, personal loans, cars) and covers your normal household needs (food, clothing, mortgage, etc.). You've been "smart" by investing 20% of your take-home pay into retirement and have a nice nest egg built, currently worth $250,000. One day, your boss calls you into his office and tells you they have to let you go because of downsizing. You must immediately figure out how to pay your bills or you are in big trouble. Cashing out your retirement costs a lot in taxes and penalties, so you don't want to go there. What do you do? Your only good option is to hope you can find another job that will pay at least as well as this one...and fast. Otherwise, you are going to have a lot of creditors calling, and the situation will go bad quickly.

Scenario 2:

Same situation as Scenario 1, except you have no debt except your mortgage. Paying off your debts, however, instead of investing 20% of your take-home pay for the three years it took you to become debt free cost you. You have only about $150,000 in your retirement fund, but you're putting 25% of your pay into retirement now to try to catch up a little bit. One day, your boss calls you into his office and tells you they have to let you go because of downsizing. You also must immediately figure out how to pay your bills. The major difference here is that you have a lot fewer of those bills to worry about. You can go find pretty much any J-O-B that pays enough to cover your basic household needs and a small mortgage while you look for something that is better for you and your family.

This idea gets at the heart of where I began this book. I don't want you to take unnecessary risks in your life. I believe that being in debt for anything except your home puts you in unnecessary risk and exponentially increases the chances of something going very wrong in your situation. If you haven't already read between the lines as I went through those examples, I do believe you should stop paying into your retirement fund while you're focused on paying off debt. This is a temporary thing–don't get lazy and waste your time getting out of debt because stopping your retirement funding while you do this does cost you! The power of compounding interest can't work for you if you're not investing so don't get lax on this. Get out of debt, and then get back to saving!

Once you're out of debt and ready to start saving again, this success principle focuses on investing wisely. The investing world is a dangerous place where you can make tons of money or lose tons of money very quickly. Since this book is more about freedom from debt, I won't spend a lot of time on investing here, but let me say this: Invest in what you understand. If you don't understand it, don't put money in it. If you want to put money in something, find someone who will teach you enough about it so you do understand it. In many places throughout scripture, the phrase, "I would not have you be ignorant..." is used. This applies here–don't be ignorant (uneducated) and, more importantly, don't be foolish!

Action Steps/Questions:

1. Which of the three success factors can you implement immediately?

2. Do you agree that it is appropriate to stop saving for retirement while focusing on paying off your debt? Why or why not?

3. Who do you know who lives like a real millionaire? Take them to lunch and discuss this chapter. I bet they'll have some interesting input for the discussion.

Chapter 10:
Point A to B:
Transportation

People are really funny about their cars. We Americans feel as though what we drive defines who we are and what we are worth. We have this notion that rich people drive only the finest automobiles and replace them every year or two. The reality is that this is the behavior of broke people. Cars hold this mysterious power as a status symbol, even though we know (at least subconsciously) that no one who makes minimum wage can afford to drive a $50,000 car. Yet if you see someone who makes next to nothing driving a shiny new BMW, you are impressed. In reality, I am too–but I'm impressed that the dealership was foolish enough to allow such people to buy something so far out of their price range! The truth is, with all the "creative financing" options available and all the payment terms out there, just about anyone can drive just about any car. So this is one of those areas that I feel it is important to discuss as a tutorial on living without debt and being smart with your money.

My Story of Stupidity

Before those of you who know me personally reprimand me for being a hypocrite, let me take a couple of paragraphs for confession. I currently drive a small pickup truck that is 18 years old at the time of this writing. It isn't fancy, but it serves its purpose as reliable transportation. I bought it with cash, the first vehicle I ever bought all on my own that way. I took a stack of $100 bills with me when I purchased it several years ago, because I had just finished a good lesson in what not to do with cars that cured my wrong thinking. Even I had to realize that my transportation was just that–transportation.

The car I had prior to that is the one where I learned my lesson. When I graduated college and got my first "real" job, I was looking to accomplish two goals: (1) buy an engagement ring for Stacy so I could propose and (2) buy a car. My car at the time had 195,000 miles on it and was starting to show signs of needing replacement. So I scrimped and saved and came up with the money to buy Stacy's ring. I started saving toward a car. But then, only five months into this new job, I got a huge promotion. My pay jumped over $10,000 per year and so I did what any self-respecting 22-year-old with a big fancy job would do–I went and bought a Mercedes. It wasn't brand new, mind you, but it was close enough and cost about $15,000 more than I could afford to buy   at the time. But...after visiting three banks, I finally found one willing to loan me the money to buy it. So here I am, ready to propose to Stacy and driving a nice, shiny car. Problem is–I now had big monthly payments to go with that car. When Stacy and I got married, I brought those payments along with me. She got a job just so we could attack that debt and get rid of the payments. It only took us 18 months to pay off that fancy car, but it also left us with no money to put toward our first home and no real savings...all for a silly car.

Here's the fun part. I really did enjoy that car, but it taught me a lesson. When it started having some mechanical problems and costing me more to keep it than it was really worth (considering I had to take it to the dealer for virtually all repairs), I sold it for $5,500 to a friend of our family. He got a car he'd always wanted (paying me cash for it), and I got $5,500 to go buy my little truck. With my stack of $100 bills, I was able to get a great deal on my truck and have a few hundred dollars left over, which was the start of our "auto maintenance/replacement fund."

Every month, we put some money into our savings strictly for use on repairing or replacing our vehicles. When Stacy's car was up for replacement a couple of years ago, I went (cash in hand) and bought her another one. I didn't have to worry about a loan; I didn't have to worry about dealing with a bank or even a finance department at a dealership. I walked in with $100 bills, counted them out, signed a few papers, and was on my merry way. Now if my truck or her car dies, we have cash in hand to go buy another one. Will I go buy another fancy Mercedes? Maybe one day. For now, it isn't in the budget, so I'll live like a millionaire and stick to what we can afford. (By the way, if you want to buy me a nice fancy car, I'd prefer a new Porsche 911 GT2–I'm just throwing that out there.)

The True Cost of a Car

Let's go car shopping. The average car payment in America is $482 per month, according to a March 2015 USA TODAY article (*http://www.usatoday.com/story/money/cars/2015/03/04/new-car-loan-record-payment/24363041/*). This means that every month, the average American pays $482 to be able to drive to and from work each day so they can make the money to be able to pay that $482 to the finance company. Follow me? Let's go buy a car the "average American can afford" based on those numbers. So we can work with real numbers, let's assume you get a 0% loan on a new car and finance it for 72 months. This means that, if your payment is $482 per month, you can borrow $34,704 ($482 x 72 months = $34,704), which is enough to cover the cost of your new mid-level Honda Accord (I chose this vehicle because they hold their resale value pretty well and the base price of a 2015 Honda Accord EX sedan, MSRP $28,946. I assume additional options, dealer fees, taxes, registration, and other items will consume the remainder of your funds (and in some states, it definitely will consume more).

As long as you never miss a payment, wreck the car too badly, or get the trade-in itch too quickly, you'll have a paid-for car in about six years, and your Honda will be worth approximately $9,000 (trade-in value; I used the Kelley Blue Book website (kbb.com) to gather this information using a 2010 Honda Accord EX sedan in good condition with 90,000 miles on it). What do most people do? They go repeat the process for a little nicer car, considering only the cost of the payments. They trade it in for another Honda, this time getting one with a few options on it. Since they got $9,000 for their trade in, they can afford to step up a little without having to increase their monthly payment.

Most people use the mentality of "how much per month?" I'm asking you to consider the mentality of "how much?" These are not even close to the same questions. A poor person wants to know if he can afford the payments; a rich person asks how much of a discount he receives for paying cash.

What if We Were Weird, Even for Just a Little While?

I could get into the discussion of why you should never buy a new car (always buy something at least two years old to take advantage of the huge depreciation (drop in value) that occurs during that first two years of a car's life). I could also get into the discussion of how you could do better than 0% APR on a car loan if you would walk in with a stack of $100 bills. Trust me, you'd be weird if you did that, and your weirdness would frighten the sales manager into giving you one sweet deal on that car. Instead, I want to assume you've already bought the new car and are paying payments on it today. So let's look at a couple of simple and smart alternative ideas for when it is time to replace your ride.

Idea 1: Keep driving it

If you can hold off on replacing your car for just a little while, it will make a huge difference. The key is to keep making payments...to yourself. Putting $482 in a savings account each month may not seem like it is a very fast road to paying cash for your next car, but hang on with me for a few minutes. Let's say you can squeeze three more years out of the car in our example once it is paid for (making it a nine-year-old car–which is nothing around the Myers house!). You've put 36 of those $482 payments away, meaning that (even without interest); you have $17,352 in the bank! Then you have two choices: go out and buy a really expensive car, putting $17,352 down and financing the rest (bad decision) or find something a couple of years old that you can pay cash for with the money you've put back. Then you can either keep saving $482 per month to work your way up to paying cash for a really nice car or, if you're like me and satisfied with driving something that isn't too expensive, you can bump down your monthly car savings to something like $200 per month.

Think about it–right now Stacy drives a reliable, decent-looking full-size car that is 7 years old. I drive a little pickup truck that has some dents and dings (it is a pickup truck!) that is almost 20 years old. Neither is in need of replacement and both are in excellent working condition.

Why replace either one? We keep driving them and keep putting back some cash.

Idea 2: Be embarrassed for a few years

If your car just absolutely is on its last legs and needs to be put down (that put a neat image in your head, didn't it?), this is the plan for you. This is also the idea I'd recommend for those just starting out who don't have any car payment, but also don't have any cash on hand to go buy something fancy. Ready? Here it is–borrow less. Yes, I am advocating that, if you cannot afford to pay cash for a car, it is okay to borrow to purchase one. But don't head to the bank just yet or get ahead of me...keep reading.

Instead of doing the "normal" thing and buying a shiny new car, let's be willing to be humble for a while and buy a $4,500 car. While we're at it, let's commit to drive that car for five years, or until the wheels fall off. Assuming you have no cash, let's also assume you finance it for one year and since it is used, you'll probably pay around 5% interest (probably no more). That means you borrowed $4,500, and at the end of one year when it is paid for, you paid roughly $4,800 (including interest and loan fees) for a car that is worth roughly $4,000 at that time.

Keep driving it! Since you committed to drive it for five years, that means you can make those $482 monthly payments to yourself for the next four years while you drive that car. Even assuming you earn no interest, you've saved over $23,000! Now you can go pay cash for a two-three-year-old car in very nice shape and repeat. You can either donate the car you've driven for those five years to a museum or a teenager just learning to drive. Either way, it will be appreciated.

My point is this: If you can be weird for just a single five-year period with your transportation, you'll never owe for another car. You can simply set aside an amount each month that fits your budget and then, whenever it is time to replace your existing car, you'll have money to do it. I've used $482 per month as an example only because it is the "average" car payment. Many of you reading this have car payments double or triple that amount, and some of you nearly passed out when I suggested you may have a payment as high as $482. Don't be so concerned with the numbers–look at the shift in behavior that is behind the numbers. Remember, this whole thing isn't about money. Now go be weird!

Action Steps

1. Do you believe what you drive says something about your value as a person? Why or why not?

2. Does the fact that I happily drive a pickup truck that is going on 20 years old make you feel like I am less worthy to provide financial advice? Why or why not?

3. What kind of car should you be driving, and are you driving something more than you can afford? Answer truthfully!

4. If you answered "yes" to question 3 above, map out a plan to step out of the cycle of indebtedness just to drive a car!

Chapter 11:
Livin' on a Prayer:
Mortgages and Housing

"Unquestionably, some people have become very rich through the use of borrowed money. However, that's also been a way to get very poor."
—Warren Buffett

I firmly believe that buying your personal residence is one of the wisest investments you can make. Even with the craziness of the housing market over the past few years, real estate has proven itself to be one of the safest and most viable places to put your money. In fact, the average middle-class American's home provides more value to his/her net worth than any other asset, including savings, retirement funding, automobiles, and just about anything else you can think of. We love our homes and they usually give us good value for our money.

Having said all that, many people go way overboard in finding and buying a home. There are many reasons for this, but I believe its genesis is found in the same logic that goes behind driving more expensive cars than we can afford. People see our homes and make a judgment about who we are and what value we have as people based on where we live.

Again referencing Dr. Thomas J. Stanley and his study of millionaires in **The Millionaire Next Door**, the average millionaire doesn't live in a mansion. They don't live in brand-new homes or even extraordinarily large homes. Instead, millionaires tend to live in a simple, older, well-maintained home in an established neighborhood. Does that sound like what you envision when you see your "dream house"? I didn't think so. But (and it is a big one)– making the wrong decision with your house purchase is one of the easiest ways to mess up an otherwise good financial plan, so read these next sections carefully and be sure to learn all you can apply to your next home purchase or refinance. By the way, if you are already in some sort of mortgage mess, please don't give up hope. There are all kinds of ways to get back on track. Don't stay in a house you can't afford and do get some guidance on how to wisely repair this misstep in your plan.

Being Ready to Take on a Mortgage

There are all kinds of mortgage products out there that will help you finance a home for your family. Most of them are simple, straightforward, and have been around for decades. Especially after the real estate meltdown of the past few years, the riskiest and most far-fetched financing ideas are losing their prestige in lieu of those that actually make mathematical sense. This is excellent news for you as a home buyer. Since this is a book about personal finance, let's discuss in some detail how much you can really afford to purchase, no matter the mortgage type you get.

If you think about all the expenses you will have as a homeowner, you should realize that owning a home is not an inexpensive proposition. You have to pay the mortgage itself, then the homeowner's insurance and property taxes and any other local taxes levied by your state/city/town/county. But don't forget about the electric bill, the water bill, cable, telephone, Internet, and other utilities. But wait, you're still not done. You have things such as yard maintenance, ongoing repairs, cleaning, association fees (in some neighborhoods), and all kinds of other miscellaneous expenses. Somehow, a young couple who walks into a bank to get pre-qualified for a loan forgets all this...and oftentimes so does the banker. You can usually get pre-qualified for 1.5 times the amount I would recommend you borrow (provided you have good credit and a decent, steady income). So before you walk into a bank or credit union to ask to be pre-qualified for a mortgage, please understand how much you can really afford.

Do you want a simple rule of thumb? The total amount of your mortgage payment on a 15-year, fixed-rate loan, plus the taxes and insurance to go along with it, should not exceed 35% of your take-home pay. Not sure about the taxes/insurance rates in your area? Then set aside 10% of the monthly payment for those and only allow the payment amount to be 25% of your take-home pay. Remember, we're looking at a 15-year, fixed-rate loan when we talk about these numbers. Let me help you a little with the math. If your total household income after all the taxes and other stuff is $5,000 per month, you should be looking for a house with a monthly payment (with taxes and insurance) of no more than $1,750.00.

$5,000 x 35% = $1,750.00

When you walk into the bank with the monthly payment figure already in your head, it will help you avoid the stupidity that looms when the bank says you're pre-qualified for way more. Any bank can back into the total amount borrowed using the monthly payment figure you provide and that will make sure you are not in over your head before you even go shopping.

What else should you do before you sign on the dotted line and buy a home?

- *Have enough in savings to put down at least 10%, but ideally 20% of the home's purchase price.* 10% down is requested for most top-notch loan products, but putting down anything less than 20% on the home's purchase price means you'll have to pay private mortgage insurance (PMI). PMI is a total waste of money that protects the mortgage company in case you don't pay. I know it sounds tough to put up 20% of the purchase price before you go buy a house, but it will save you about $40 per month per $100,000 borrowed. The rules and laws around PMI are a bit complicated, but be aware that if you don't put 20% down, you should expect to have to pay PMI until you have paid the loan down to where you "own" at least 20% of the home. If you can avoid PMI by putting down 20%, do it!

- *Be debt free (or very close).* Remember the very first words of the introduction to this book Let me remind you: "Debt equals risk and there is no exception to that equation." The more debt you have, the more risk you have that something will go wrong and make a mess for you financially. If you are struggling now to pay your bills, you are definitely not in any shape to buy a house. There is nothing wrong with renting a house or apartment, and there are many very bad things that can (and likely will) happen if you buy a house when you aren't able to control your debt. It is akin to the couple who are fighting all the time so they decide to have a baby, thinking the pregnancy and new baby will solve all their marital problems. If you're a parent, you know better than that!

- *Have a good emergency fund built up.* Trust me, you will have some unexpected expenses the moment you sign the paperwork on your "new" house. You'll find out the "new" house has some "old" stuff that will need to be repaired/replaced. You'll find there is this beautiful decorating item that absolutely must *cough* be purchased to complete the living room décor. You'll find a crack in the foundation. Something is going to happen, and it is going to cost money.

Common Mortgage Types and How They Work

Now that I've scared you away from buying a house, let's talk about a couple of the ways you can finance a home and see if I can get you back into willingness to consider making a purchase. Mortgages can be placed into two major categories: Fixed Rate Mortgages and Adjustable Rate Mortgages (ARMs). Both products allow you to borrow a set amount and pay back payments over a set amount of time, using an amortization schedule to outline how much each payment will be and how much of that payment will go to principal (actual borrowed amount) and how much will go to interest. Don't worry, an amortization schedule is not a complicated creature–it is just a table of numbers that clearly indicate how much of your payment each month goes toward which component of the loan (principal, interest, or something else). You can find amortization calculators and amortization schedule generators all over the Internet, so don't be scared by that term.

There are many other types of mortgage loan products out there, including interest only mortgages, negative amortization loans, balloon payment mortgages, and graduated payment mortgages. Since these are less common and products that I recommend that you avoid anyway, let's focus on the two major types.

Fixed Rate Mortgages

A fixed rate mortgage is the simplest of all basic mortgage types. As you may have gathered by its name, the "fixed rate" in the title is referring to the interest rate on the loan. A fixed rate mortgage will have a static (unchanging) interest rate for the life of the loan. Loan terms can vary greatly, but the most common scenarios are 15-year, 20-year, or 30-year fixed mortgages. This means that the borrowed amount will be paid back over a 15-, 20-, or 30-year term, respectively. Unfortunately, you can't just divide the amount borrowed on a 15-year mortgage by 180 and figure out the monthly payment (15 years x 12 months per year = 180). That's where an amortization schedule comes into play. Let's assume you get a 15-year, $100,000 mortgage at a 5% interest rate with no points (points are pre-paid interest). On this loan, you should expect payments of about $791.00 per month, based on a quick calculation I performed on a financial calculator. You would pay these same payments every single month for 180 months (15 years) at which point the loan is paid in full. If you pay extra toward principal, the payments do not change, but the loan is paid off faster.

There are two common (albeit becoming less common) land mines you need to avoid when working with fixed rate mortgages:

- **Points**–Also sometimes called "discount points," points are simply pre-paid interest. One Point = 1% of the borrowed amount. You may see a loan advertised with a 2.75% APR with 3 points. This means that you will have to pay the lender 3% of the total amount borrowed up front to get the 2.75% interest rate on that loan. This is a widespread practice and one that many people just don't think about. They assume it is part of the "required" closing costs so they just pay it. I don't think you should pay points and even though it is a common practice to pay points to reduce the overall interest rate on the loan, this is a gamble that may or may not come out to your advantage. Keep it simple and don't pay points if you can avoid them.

- *Pre-pay penalties*–Banks don't like people like me. I don't borrow money but, if I do, I don't take long to pay it back. When I pay it back too fast, they don't get all the interest payments they hoped for. Thus, many mortgage products will include a pre-payment penalty. All that means is if you happen to pay back the mortgage early (by paying extra payments), they are going to charge you a fee when the loan gets paid off early. I hope it goes without saying that this is something to avoid. If you end up getting a huge raise and want to pay off your house 10 years early, you shouldn't be penalized for it! A loan that has a pre-payment penalty also usually has some other catch or other dangerous aspect to it, so my general advice is to avoid any loan product that includes any sort of pre-payment penalty.

Adjustable Rate (ARM) and terms

Adjustable Rate Mortgages are huge when interest rates are high and falling because, as the name suggests, the interest rate adjusts periodically based on market conditions. You will commonly see ARMs shown something like 3/1 or 5/1, which simply means that for the first X number of years the rate is fixed, and then thereafter it will adjust each year. For example, a 3/1 ARM will have a fixed rate for three years, then adjust one time per year every year thereafter for the remaining life of the loan. Like a fixed rate mortgage, these loans will still have something like a 15- or 30-year term for full repayment of the loan; the only difference is that the payment will change based on the interest rate's change.

How does the interest rate change? Excellent question! It depends on the index the rate adjustment is tied to and the margin percentage that is written into the loan. Confused yet? Let's break it down a little. While there are several financial indexes out there, the most common one is LIBOR, which stands for "London InterBank Offering Rate."". LIBOR is the average lending rates from several of the major banks in London, England. It is a frequently-used measure of the current international interest rates. The margin is a figure that stays constant and provides a padding or margin (hence the name) for the lender to always be able to make money as the rates adjust.

Let's look at a quick example that may help you understand the terms a bit. Let's assume you get a 5/1 ARM with a 2% margin. If today's LIBOR rate is 3.5%, then you could expect a 5-year fixed rate of 5.5% (LIBOR + margin). Five years later, the rate will adjust. The lender will look at the LIBOR rate, which let's assume has risen to 3.8%. Your new rate on the loan, fixed for the next year, is now 5.8%. The next year, this process repeats, and repeats every year until the loan is paid off. Your payment adjusts upward or downward to reflect the change in interest rate.

If you've not already gathered it, the primary intent of an ARM is to transfer the risk of higher interest rates to you. Rather than the bank giving you a 15-year fixed loan and taking on all the risk of an interest rate increase, they pass that risk along to you. Why would you take an ARM then? Because usually the up-front interest rate on an ARM is slightly lower than that on a fixed rate loan and sometimes you can even pay interest only for a certain period of time. This means that, at first, your payments could be substantially lower. This is a bad idea because you only pay interest. Since they can qualify for a bigger house because the payment is initially lower, however, many people find this type of mortgage very appealing. Remember, though, that you have taken on all the risk of the interest rate changes. As way too many homeowners learned in the most recent economic crash, if your rate adjusts higher, you may end up with a house you can no longer afford.

My Take on It All

As you probably have gathered by reading this chapter thus far, I am a fan of the boring approach. I believe that, should you need to take out a loan to purchase your home, there are some strict guidelines to follow to ensure you don't get in over your head and take the route that will get your home paid for most quickly. My simple rules for a mortgage are:

- If you must get a loan, get no more than a 15-year, fixed-rate mortgage.
- Don't allow your entire monthly PITI payment (PITI stands for Principal, Interest, Taxes, Insurance) to exceed 35% of your take-home pay. If you are not sure how much taxes and insurance will be, then shop using a principal + interest payment figure that doesn't exceed 25% of your take-home pay.
- Get pre-qualified before you go shopping.
- If your credit is not very good, either clean it up by behaving over time or seek out manual underwriting for your loan.

- Don't pay any points if you can avoid them. Realize that paying points is simply paying interest in advance and is something you can usually negotiate away.
- Avoid any loan product (in fact, avoid any company altogether) that has a pre-payment penalty.
- Pay off your mortgage early. So what if there are tax benefits associated with keeping a mortgage–the math on those doesn't work and the benefits of owning your home free and clear win out anyway. Don't pay it off early at the expense of your retirement savings, but if there is extra money coming in, take advantage of it and pay down your mortgage balance.
- More on these topics can be found in the chapter on why "I Don't Care About Your Credit Score...and You Shouldn't Either."

Reverse Mortgage

Even though this falls a bit outside the range of a normal discussion of mortgages, I do want to take a little time to talk about reverse mortgages. These products are popular for those who are a little older and own their home (or have a lot of equity in it). A reverse mortgage is, as the name suggests, a product by which a lender pays you payments each month and "buys" your house while you are still living in it. There are some perks, such as the monthly tax-free payments from the lender. You also get to live there while you are "selling" your home. That's why it is so popular among the older generation who may want to use the equity in their home for medical expenses or other desired expenditures.

The problem with reverse mortgages is that you are selling your home! You are putting a paid-for home at risk in the name of having some money now. Another major concern is related to the various fees that are tied to these products. Because the lender is not going to lose money as a matter of practice on its dealings, the fee structure on these products is usually very painful for you. You can expect to find title fees, origination fees, mortgage insurance fees, appraisals, flood certifications, as well as many other potential "gotcha" fees along the way. In addition, because the elderly are the most common targets of these types of products, wrongdoers have found this an excellent market in which to commit fraud. In fact, the Federal Trade Commission states that reverse mortgages have a greater fraud risk than any other mortgage product in existence. That is enough to keep me away.

Action Steps/Questions

1. Using what you learned in this chapter, calculate how much of a house payment you should be able to make comfortably, given your income.

2. How far off is the figure you just calculated in question 1 from your actual house payment? If it is a great deal off, what steps can you take to bring things into balance?

Chapter 12:
I Don't Care About Your Credit Score...and You Shouldn't Either

"Not everything that can be counted counts, and not everything that counts can be counted."
–Albert Einstein

Since you've read this far, I figure I might as well be blunt about it: I really don't care how good or bad your credit score is. I don't care if you've done everything in your power to have some elite status with the credit bureaus that make lenders fall down and worship at your feet as you walk into the bank. I don't care if lenders laugh at the thought of processing your next loan application. I can't say it any more plainly than this: I truly do not care if you have good credit or bad credit because credit is not our goal. Feel free to stop reading for a moment so that can sink in. I really want you to think long and hard about my statement about your credit score because, for many of you, this rocks your very foundation. It goes against everything you've read, everything you've been told, and likely everything you believe about being a good person.

Now that you've recovered from your shock, let me explain why your credit score isn't important to me and why it shouldn't be important to you, either. Please don't misunderstand me–having a good credit score doesn't hurt anything and can in fact help some things. Having a good credit score means you've behaved with your debt. It means you've had enough debt for the credit bureaus to take notice. It also means you've borrowed enough money over the course of some time to establish (at least to their scoring system) that you like having some debt and enjoy paying payments. Please notice before we go any further that I didn't say, "I don't care about your credit report." I care very much that you ensure your report is complete, accurate, and as good as it should be. I'll explain a bit more about that shortly. Your credit report is a document that you should review periodically with a focus on ensuring that the data presented is correct and to make sure any errors are cleared up in a timely manner.

Having a good credit score is not a moral issue. It does not make you a substandard man or woman to have a bad credit score, just as having a good credit score doesn't make you above anyone else. Despite what lenders would have you believe, you do not have to make every effort in your human powers to improve your score. Instead, you simply need to behave with your money. Your credit score will take care of itself. Did you get that? Don't make efforts to improve your credit score and please (please) never do anything with the sole motivation of improving your credit score because that is aiming for the wrong target. Your target is financial success. Your credit score tells lenders how likely you are to pay them back if you borrow money. Since with what I'm teaching you, you'll no longer be borrowing money, your credit score shouldn't matter too much. See where I'm going here?

I know some of you are saying, "yeah, but…," so before you get carried away, let me make three concessions that will make you feel a little better about what you've been taught all these years:

1. Having a good credit score makes it easier to borrow money (duh).

If you are looking to purchase a home, I won't get upset with you if you go get a 15-year, fixed-rate mortgage with a payment that is no more than 35% of your take-home pay. It is the only form of debt I have no problem with when used in strict moderation. Having a good credit score will help you find a lower interest rate on that mortgage. It will also help you find more lenders who are willing to work with you. You can also be assured of a bit less hassle at the overall shopping process because you can get pre-approved for a decent rate in advance and be aware of what your budget allows based on the real payment you can afford. Note: Be careful because banks will almost always pre-qualify you for much more than you should actually borrow on a home, so –be realistic about what you can afford and shop based on that number instead of the bank's inflated idea of what you can borrow.

For those of you who have a poor credit score and can't get a home mortgage because of it, maybe you need to rent a bit longer while you clean up some of your financial behaviors. We'll talk in a bit about how long things stay on your report and what that means. If you had one serious event (major illness, for instance) that wiped you out and thus wreaked havoc on your score, you should consider looking at the option of manual underwriting. A "normal" mortgage lender will pull your credit report, look at the score, and use a simple table of numbers to determine how much you can borrow based on your income and your credit score. A manual underwriter will pull your report and call you or invite you to his/her office to discuss what happened that caused these issues. There is a bigger hassle factor in going through manual underwriting, but it is a good solution for those who have a good explanation for a poor credit score. To find a mortgage lender that does manual underwriting in your area, just call around. You're usually going to have better success with smaller banks and/or credit unions with this.

2. Having a poor credit score can affect your ability to get a job or serve in certain capacities.

For example, if you have bad credit, you can lose your security clearance levels in the military. You can be withdrawn from consideration as a job candidate. In some instances, this makes sense. If you have a poor credit score, it indicates to potential employers that you cannot manage your money. The fact is (in their collective opinion), if you can't manage your money well enough to pay bills on time, you likely aren't going to be a very good employee. Notice that they are using your credit score to judge your character. If you'll behave with your money instead of worrying about your credit score, this issue won't be a concern.

3. Having a good credit score can reduce your rates on insurance.-

Insurance companies measure risk for a living. They have to make an educated guess as to whether or not you're going to cost them money and base the rates they charge you largely on that. It only makes sense that they would consider your credit score to determine some simple risk factors about you. If you walk in and ask them to insure your car, home, or business and they pull a credit report that shows them you can't pay your bills each month, chances are they feel you are a higher risk in other categories as well. Just like point #2, you are being judged for potential risk because of your behavior with debt. If you will behave with money, in general, this won't be an issue either.

What a Credit Report Actually Is

Simply put, your credit report contains information about your borrowing and repayment history. More specifically, your credit report will display all of the loans you've taken, where the loan came from, and any repayment details. Along with each of those loans, your credit report will contain information on whether or not you have been late on any payments in the past, including how late you were. This is registered in 30-day increments, so a bill that was paid 38 days late will list as a 30-day delinquency, a bill that was paid 141 days late will list as a 120-day delinquency, and so forth. You will also find current and previous address information, social security number(s), and details on any requests to view your credit report (called "inquiries").

Your report will break down your borrowing into the two major types of loans: installment loans and revolving credit. Mortgages and car loans are installment loans–this type of loan has a set amount you've borrowed up front with the expectation of paying back a set monthly payment for a set number of months to pay back the loan balance. Credit cards are the most common type of revolving credit. This type of loan allows you a credit limit that provides you a pre-authorized amount you can borrow on that loan while giving you the freedom to borrow or not borrow that amount at your leisure. Assuming any amount is owed when a bill is scheduled to be generated (sometimes called the "billing date," "statement date" or "cycle date"), a bill is sent to you with a calculated minimum payment and interest charge. The payment is based on the balance of that loan at the time the bill is generated.

Why is there a distinction between installment and revolving loans on your report? Consider this: If I'm a potential lender reviewing your credit report, I'm going to be looking at your current debt load (how much you have in debt right now), plus I'm going to be very interested in how much debt you could easily take on through active revolving accounts. Since you can't borrow more money on an existing installment loan, lenders don't look too heavily at those for considering your capacity to carry additional debt. For example, your only installment loan may be a small car loan, but you may have five active credit cards with a credit limit of $20,000 available on each. This means that with no questions asked, you could charge $100,000 in a single month. As a potential lender, I am definitely going to consider this when assessing risk. .

There are lots of other interesting pieces of information lenders review, such as your debt-to-income ratio (how much debt you have vs. how much income you have each month to pay payments on those debts), your past delinquencies (late payments), etc. All of the information presented on your report rolls into a credit score, which is what most lenders use as the focal point of their decision-making. We'll talk more about how your score is calculated in a bit.

Understand and Ensure Accuracy of Your Report

Let's talk a little about who compiles your credit data into a formal "credit report" and for what purposes. There are three major consumer credit reporting agencies (or CRAs):

- Equifax (*http://www.equifax.com*)
- Experian (*http://www.experian.com*)
- TransUnion (*http://www.transunion.com*)

Each of these reporting agencies compiles and publishes virtually the same data for consumers and their behaviors with debt. They are also governed by the same laws and standards for reporting. So what's the difference? For our purposes, there really isn't any. Each reporting agency does have its own scoring method to provide a credit score, and each company has a unique name for its version of your credit score, but since we're worried about the report rather than the score, we won't spend much time on the differences. I do want to outline for you how the score (in general) is calculated from all three agencies because it will help you develop a clearer understanding of why your score is all about debt.

No matter the credit reporting agency, each uses a variation of the FICO (Fair Isaac & Company; *http://www.fico.com*) scoring system, introduced in 1956. This scoring system is closely guarded and has been tweaked frequently over the years so that no one (at least publicly) knows exactly how it works.

FICO does provide some information about how it determines your score, with as many details as they'll publicly release available at a summary page on their website.

The best representation of this is the graph on that web page provided here for reference. As you can see, FICO looks at five categories when determining your score:

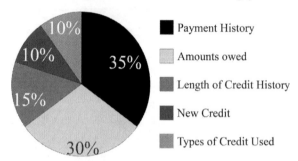

- *Payment History (35%)*–This section considers whether or not you have paid all accounts as agreed or whether you've been past due, filed bankruptcy, or had other issues with paying all your debt accounts. In other words, this section looks to answer the question of whether you are paying back your debts as promised.
- *Amounts Owed (30%)*–This section looks at how much you owe on the various types of debts you have (installment and revolving). It also looks at the percentage of the available credit you're using (it is a red flag to have several maxed-out credit cards, for example). In other words, this section looks to answer the question of how heavily burdened you are by debt.
- *Length of Credit History (15%)*–This section is one of the easiest to understand. How long have you had debt and how long has it been since you used that debt by making purchases?
- *New Credit (10%)*–This section seeks to determine whether you are on the path to taking out lots of new loans, as this is a red flag. It looks at the number of recent credit inquiries, how many accounts you've

recently opened (also vs. how many accounts you've had for a long time), etc. In simplest terms, this section looks to answer the question of whether or not you are seeking out new debt and, if so, how much and for what purpose?

- Types of Credit Used (10%)–This section is a bit mysterious. According to FICO, this section looks at the number and the types of accounts you have. Exactly how this is factored into the score is unknown, but most agree that FICO is trying to ensure you have a balance of debt types to balance your overall risk as a borrower.

FICO openly admits that these percentages are general guidelines and that, for some groups of individuals (they provide the example of someone who hasn't had credit for very long), the weights assigned may be different. So even though I've spent some time outlining these details for you, please understand that these are no more than general guidelines and FICO docs not openly share any additional details. Knowing what goes into your score, many people then want to know what a "good score" is. For that sake, I'll provide you a quick summary of that data.

FICO scores range between 300-850 A score of 740 or above is considered excellent, while a score of 600 or below is considered poor Much lower than 600 and you will struggle to get a loan of any sort (is that a bad thing?).

Let's look back at those five FICO scoring categories for a moment. Notice something obvious about them all? You hopefully see that every one of those categories is only concerned with debt (borrowing). If you never borrow money, you can't have a good FICO score. If you don't pay payments on something, FICO is confused. This is why I don't really care about your credit score. I don't want you to borrow money, and your credit score can only reflect information when you borrow.

Since your credit report may impact more than your ability to borrow money and because your credit report is a great way to learn quickly if fraud has been committed in your name, I don't want you to be unnecessarily negatively impacted by an error on the report. The credit reporting agencies are only responsible to report information–they don't necessarily guarantee its accuracy because they only report the information that lenders provide to them. If the lender provides inaccurate information, your credit report will contain inaccurate information. It really is that simple.

What is your responsibility? First and foremost, you need to know that you should pull your credit report from each of the three major credit reporting agencies about once each year and review it for accuracy. Based on the Fair and Accurate Credit Transactions Act of 2003 (more commonly referred to as the FACT Act), which amended the Fair Credit Reporting Act (FCRA), you are legally allowed to obtain a free copy of your credit report from each of the three major reporting agencies. This act also called for the creation of a one-stop website to allow you to access all three reports, *http://www.annualcreditreport. com*. This website is directly linked to all three reporting agencies and allows you to access your reports for free. Not only can you view the reports online, but you can also print the reports, file a dispute on any items you find to be in error (this is very important and a huge improvement of the process of the past), and if you feel it is necessary, you can pay a small fee to see your credit score. Although there are numerous websites out there that enable you to review your credit report and get your score, this is the only one I recommend you use because it is specifically designed for you to get your report for free and highly regulated to ensure it stays that way.

If you are uncomfortable dealing with an online credit report, you can also request your report for free from each of the agencies using postal mail. To do so, you can access the printable form online from the Federal Trade Commission (FTC) at the following web address: *http:// www.ftc.gov/bcp/edu/resources/forms/requestformfinal. pdf.* Once you've printed the form, simply follow the provided instructions and expect to receive your free credit report(s) within a few weeks. Similarly, if you find any of your information to be inaccurate, you can also file a dispute through the postal mail. Currently, the addresses for the dispute departments of the three major CRAs are:

Equifax P.O. Box 7404256 Atlanta, GA 30374-0256	Experian Dispute Department P.O. Box 9701 Allen, TX 75013	TransUnion Consumer Solutions P.O. Box 2000 Chester, PA 19022-2000

I've also provided a copy of a sample dispute letter in the Appendix in the back of this book.

Action Steps/Questions

1. Access and review your credit report from at least one of the three major credit reporting agencies using *http://www.annualcreditreport.com.*

2. Dispute any inaccuracies you find in your report and take care of any items that require attention (cancel an old, unused credit card, update your outdated personal information, etc.).

Chapter 13:
Credit and Debt Law:
Some Basics

I spent six years working for the credit card division of one of the world's largest financial institutions. I started in the collections department, calling people who were past due on their bills to attempt to work out some sort of payment arrangements. From there, I moved into training people how to collect. Next, I became an instructional designer, actually developing the training materials and methods used to teach collectors (and many other credit card-related divisions) how to do their jobs most effectively. It was a valuable education for me because I can now share many of the details about how credit and debt laws work and give you the information that will actually help you be better informed about what laws and regulations matter when it comes to your debt without overwhelming you with a lot of extra legalese and other unnecessary details. If you are in debt, this chapter alone is worth every penny you paid for this book.

There are four federal regulations that I believe make up the bulk of the information you need to be familiar with as a debtor:

- Fair Debt Collection Practices Act (FDCPA)
- Fair Credit Reporting Act (FCRA)
- Fair and Accurate Credit Transactions Act (FACT Act or FACTA)
- Credit Card Accountability Responsibility and Disclosure Act of 2009 (Credit CARD Act of 2009)

We will spend some time on each of them individually, but you will also find that they work together (and even overlap in some instances). If you are in any trouble with your debts, you should become familiar with these four regulations and make notes regarding how they can most effectively protect you. Keep in mind also that there are numerous other laws that apply to debt and collections, such as the Truth in Lending Act (TILA), the Consumer Credit Protection Act (CCPA, to which the FDCPA which we will discuss is closely tied), etc.

All of these laws are broken every single day by collectors all over the nation. If you know your rights and their responsibilities, I promise it will work in your favor. You also should do a little online research and determine if your state offers additional protections for you as it relates to being in debt. For example, during my tenure in collections, Massachusetts had some of the most specific and stringent collections laws in the nation, providing additional protections above and beyond the federal regulations.

Disclaimer

Even though I've provided you some background about my qualifications to discuss this subject, let me add that laws change regularly and that there are numerous state regulations that often trump federal ones. In addition, your specific situation may be unique due to innumerable specific facts that I cannot know or address. Please understand, then, that even though this information is valid, it may or may not provide a complete picture of your situation, and I strongly advise you to learn additional information if necessary to tackle your debts.

The Federal Fair Debt Collection Practices Act (FDCPA) was enacted in 1978 to provide a structure for collectors to use in using fair and appropriate practices in the collection of personal debts and to reduce the abusive collections practices within the industry. The FDCPA set up specific guidelines for debt collection practices, more clearly defined the rights of consumers involved with debt collectors, and outlined the penalties associated with a collector who violates the law.

Let me start by pointing out that FDCPA specifically outlines the rules for third party collectors (collection agencies) and not directly for the creditor from which you borrowed the money.

I know that is a little confusing, so let me clarify. If you borrowed money from Bank X and Bank X calls to collect, the FDCPA does not necessarily directly apply to them (they are a first party collector). If, however, Bank X hires Collection Agency Y to do its collections, Collection Agency Y must follow FDCPA. Because it actually makes for good industry practice, however, it has become standard protocol among most major companies that engage in collecting debts to follow FDCPA as their guideline Also, some state laws do outline that first party collectors must follow FDCPA. It is also important to note that FDCPA regulations are specific to consumer debts. Business debts, along with many personal debts incurred for business purposes, are generally not covered under FDCPA rules.

The FDCPA outlines a long list of prohibited behaviors, all of which are related to more clearly defining what constitutes abuse or deception in the practices of collectors. Some of the more noteworthy items on this list are:

- **Hours of contact:** A collector may call someone only between the hours of 8:00 am and 9:00 pm (based on the consumer's time zone).
- **Use of Profanity or Abusive Language:** A collector may not use any language that is clearly abusive or profane in their attempts to get you to pay (this is one of many sections in the FDCPA that is somewhat subjective).
- **Calling at Work:** A collector can call you at work but must stop doing so if advised that the consumer may not receive such calls at his/her workplace.
- **Misrepresentation:** A collector must be honest in his dealings with you. For instance, he cannot claim to be an attorney.
- **Cease and Desist:** If you tell a collector he/she may no longer contact you by telephone, the collector must cease all such contact. Note: Although the FDCPA dictates this request must be made in writing, several state laws allow a verbal notification to suffice.

The FDCPA also provides some specific duties that any collector must perform during any contact, such as correctly and appropriately identifying themselves. There are numerous other guidelines in the regulation, and if you are looking for some good night-time reading material on a night in which you're struggling to fall asleep, I encourage you to read the full text of the FDCPA, which is available from the Federal Trade Commission (the regulating agency with oversight for the FDCPA) at *http:// www.ftc.gov/bcp/edu/pubs/consumer/credit/cre27.pdf.*

If you find a collector is misbehaving, having some knowledge of the FDCPA and providing a legitimate threat to report his misbehavior to the FTC will go a long way to protecting your rights.

FCRA & FACTA

The Fair Credit Reporting Act (FCRA) works very closely with the FDCPA to provide the guidelines for the appropriate use of consumer information, especially as related to their credit reporting. Given the name of the law, I bet you didn't see that one coming! This law has changed a few times since its initial passage in 1970, with the most recent major change occurring in 2003 with the addition to the FCRA of the Fair and Accurate Credit Transactions Act (FACT Act). The FACT Act established the requirement for credit reporting agencies to provide you a free copy of your credit report once per year as well as the online venue (*http://www.annualcreditreport.com*) for accessing that report. Since we've discussed the FACT Act and its provisions in some detail in the chapter about your credit report and score, I won't focus on that section of the law here. Instead, let's look at a few of the other important aspects of the law.

One of the biggest provisions in the FCRA is the standardization of the time frames for which negative information can remain on your credit report and thus be reflected in your credit score. Here is a brief list:

- Bankruptcy (Chapter 7)–10 years from the date of filing[2]
- Bankruptcy (Chapter 13)–7 years from the date of filing[1]

---

2 See Chapter 15, "I Give Up–Bankruptcy," for more information on the difference between these two types of bankruptcy.

- Tax Liens–7 years from the date they are paid
- Judgments–7 years from the date of judgment
- Delinquencies (of any level)–7 years from the date of delinquency

As you can see, the standard for the most common types of negative reportings is seven years from the date of the negative event. It is true that some things will fall off sooner, and it is also true that some things will take longer (although you can contact the credit reporting agency and have it removed once these time frames have passed). There are also state laws that come into play, especially if there is some sort of dispute. These general guidelines will, however, help you understand why I am suspicious of anyone who claims to be able to improve your credit score or to clean up your report. Legally, the FCRA provides a pretty solid set of rules for how these reportings work.

Another important provision of the FCRA is to outline the specific purposes for which someone (or some business) can legitimately access your credit information. This is the law that provides potential employers the right to use your credit file in determining your eligibility for employment with their company. This is also the law that allows insurance companies to use your credit report to determine your risk level, etc. In other words, the FCRA provides the guidelines under which someone can use your credit report to assess your character.

One more and very important change that came to the FCRA through the passage of the FACT Act is the set of guidelines that helped increase protection against identity theft. This is the law that requires protection of your personal information and secure disposal of all no-longer-needed credit information. Additionally, the FACT Act set up a formal set of credit alerts that all credit reporting agencies and creditors must recognize. For example, if you are the victim of identity theft, you can request that an alert be placed on your credit bureau report to reflect this and thus make it more difficult for someone to gain access by requiring more stringent verification. Also, if you are a military service person who is deployed, your credit file can be noted with this information to help prevent identity theft in your name while you are absent and unable to deal with the issue.

One last provision we'll discuss is the guideline it establishes in the case of a credit dispute. Since you know you should access your credit report annually and review it for accuracy and completeness, here's what to do if there is a problem: Dispute it! In the chapter regarding your credit score, I gave you the details on how to dispute online or by mail (see the Appendix for the dispute form letter). The FCRA details that once you notify a credit reporting agency that there is an error on your report, they have 30 days to either resolve the dispute or to remove the information from your report entirely. There is a clause that allows more time if there is further investigation required, but since the process of disputes is pretty automated, this is not as common an occurrence as you might think.

Since I have provided a very simplistic look into the FCRA and the FACT Act in the preceding paragraphs, I would encourage you to review the full law if you are experiencing an issue related to what you think the FCRA may cover. If you would like to read the full text of the FCRA (including the amendment that includes the FACT Act), it is available from the Federal Trade Commission (FTC), the governing agency tasked with oversight of the regulation, at *http://www.ftc.gov/os/statutes/031224fcra. pdf.*

Credit C.A.R.D. Act of 2009

The Credit Card Accountability Responsibility and Disclosure Act of 2009 (better known as the Credit CARD Act of 2009) was set up in response to much of the infidelity of major banks as a result of the financial meltdown in 2007-2008. In the news, there was a lot made of the "Credit Cardholders' Bill of Rights." The Credit CARD Act of 2009 includes much of the framework of that recommended Bill of Rights, as well as many other provisions. Most of the detail of the bill relates to how a credit card company must disclose information to you and sought to end many of the predatory behaviors of the past, such as:

• Raising your credit limit without advance notification
• Providing a vague or no explanation of how your minimum payment is allocated
• Charging too many fees for things such as going over the credit limit
• Targeting teenagers and young college students to sign up for credit cards

There are numerous protections for consumers in this bill, and I would encourage you to review some of those protections. The Wikipedia article about this act (*http:// en.wikipedia.org/wiki/Credit_CARD_Act_of_2009*) provides an excellent overview of the provisions so you can see them in bullet-point form. As you review the act or its summary, I want you to see how dangerous credit cards can be. Look at the colossal mess the government had to step in and stop or at least attempt to regulate! If you are not in credit card debt, it will be a great motivator to stay out. If you're already in the mess of credit card debt, it will help you understand some of the traps credit card companies may have set for you. If you find yourself wanting more information, the full legislation can be found at the Federal Trade Commission's (FTC) website at *http://www.ftc.gov/ogc/stat3/credit-card-pub-l-111-24. pdf.*

Action Steps/Questions

1. True or false: A collector can call you at your place of employment? Which regulation governs this practice?

2. List at least three provisions found in the Credit CARD Act of 2009.

3. How long does a credit reporting agency have to resolve a dispute you file before they must remove it entirely from your report?

4. What protections are you afforded with the implementation of the FACT Act if you are a victim of identity theft?

Chapter 14:
Debt Management and CCCS

I hope that you are reading this chapter strictly for the educational benefit it will provide. If not, it likely means you feel you are over your head in debt and unsure what to do. You've probably heard about these companies on TV, radio, the Internet, or in a magazine somewhere that will help reduce your debts, get you back on track, and improve your credit score. This chapter is all about understanding what debt management and consumer credit counseling is and whether or not it is a good choice for you based on your situation.

First off, you need to understand clearly that debt management companies are not some magical entity that will miraculously fix all your credit problems and make your life easy. They are also not able to improve your credit score by sprinkling some credit fairy dust or waving a magic wand. These companies serve a legitimate purpose, but please don't get caught up in the hype they try to sell. Even though many of the agencies are considered not-for-profit, they will generally expect you to pay them for their services and will make money for what they do.

Why all the hype? I think it is sort of like the hype that car dealers feel necessary to try to sell you your next car. I don't know about you, but if I need another car, I'm not more motivated to go buy it by poor acting, scam-like promotions or other gimmicks. Yet every minute of every day, you can flip through the channels and find a terrible commercial trying to sell you a car. So let's just know there is a lot of hype in all the advertising for debt management agencies and recognize it for what it is–advertising.

So what is the real selling point of debt management companies? Simplicity and convenience. There are two main approaches a debt management company may take when trying to reduce your debts: (1) work with your creditors to reduce the interest rate and/or required minimum payment amount on your debts or (2) battle your creditors to take a debt settlement (accept an amount to pay off the balance in full for an amount less than that). The first approach isn't bad; the second is quite dangerous, if for no other reason than it can wreak havoc on your credit, cost you a lot in fees, and require you to pay taxes you didn't expect to have to pay. Like companies that promote reverse mortgages, companies that offer to help you by taking the debt settlement approach should put you on high alert. This arena is full of fraud and chock full of extremely high fees.

No matter the approach your debt settlement company attempts to sell you, recognize that all they are really selling is simplicity and convenience. They can handle the hassle for you and guide you through it. All you do is sign some paperwork and give them money; they deal with everything else. This is not a bad selling point, but don't stop reading yet.

A debt management company can be organized as a for-profit or not-for-profit entity. The methods they use for working through your debt have little to do with the way they are organized, but the success rates are much higher and the fraud rates and fee structures much lower with the not-for-profit agencies. To give you some perspective, at the time of this writing, American Express, Chase, and Discover won't even work with for-profit agencies because of problems associated with them. The message that you should take away: if you decide to work with debt management, work with one that is not-for-profit.

I know, I know, some of you are reading this and saying, "Oh no! I am already working with one of these companies...what should I do?!"Well, even though I don't work in the Human Resources division of any company, I have to give the standard HR answer here–"it depends." If you're working with a for-profit agency, you need to be informed about their practices, your contract with the agency, and what fees, etc. you are responsible for. The best way to do that is to review your paperwork with the agency, then find out if they are accredited. If they are not accredited, you are likely stuck with whatever details are in your contract with them. If they are accredited, you need to learn a bit about the accrediting agency. For for-profit agencies, there are two: The Association of Settlement Companies (TASC, *http://www.tascsite.org/*) and United States Organizations for Bankruptcy Alternatives (USOBA, *http://www.usoba.org/*). These two accrediting agencies have good information on their websites about how their member agencies should be behaving. If you find something out of line, you should call the agency on it and, if possible, get out of your relationship with them.

Not-for-profit debt management companies, often referred to as Consumer Credit Counseling Services or CCCS, can perform the same functions as the agencies that are for-profit. The major exception is that not-for-profit agencies don't usually focus on trying to settle your debts. They instead usually follow the practice of working out a debt management plan (DMP) with your creditors. This means they contact your creditors and attempt to lower your monthly minimum payment and interest rates. Once qualified, you write a single check to the debt management company to cover all your debt payments in their plan, and they distribute the funds to your creditors. When I worked in collections, our standard procedure when someone qualified with CCCS was to automatically reduce their interest rate to 9.99% fixed (down from a rate that was sometimes as high as 28.99%) and recalculate the minimum payment based on that lower interest rate. Once they were qualified with CCCS, the process was pretty automatic from our side. So as you can see, there are benefits to being with a debt management company.

There are some accrediting agencies that also oversee not-for-profit debt management agencies. They provide oversight, accreditation, and education for member agencies. The two accrediting associations are the National Federation for Credit Counselors (NFCC, *http:// www.nfcc.org/*) and the Association of Independent Consumer Credit Counseling Agencies (AICCCA, *http:// www.aiccca.org/*). If you plan on working with a not-for-profit agency, ensure they are certified by at least one of these accrediting agencies.

So you've read this far and seen there are some dangers, but you conclude that debt management companies can be a pretty good idea if you're drowning in debt. So what's the downside? I could give you several, but let me focus on my top three. These are reason enough for me to advise 95% of people reading this book to avoid a debt management agency:

- ***You can get lazy***–I don't want the process of your getting out of debt to be super easy. If everything happens to go perfectly with your debt management plans, I don't want you to say, "...all I had to do was write a check and four years later I'm debt free." That, to me, sounds just like saying, "...all I had to do was pay my tuition and four years later they gave me my degree." You should fight, struggle, and beat your debt. Otherwise, you may go back into debt, and I promise getting out is not easier the second time around.

- *Missing a Payment = Huge Mess*–Without getting into the possibilities of credit reporting problems, late fees or other issues, debt management companies don't perform flawlessly. If you don't pay them on time, they don't pay your creditors on time. What can this mean for you? If you can't come up with the big lump sum payment by the due date set by the debt management company, you may be looking at being past due on every single bill in the plan for that month. Ouch. This can mean big problems and even result in your being dropped from the program by the creditor. This can create all sorts of messes for you, and your debt management company isn't going to be very sympathetic. By the same token, you must always be ready to pay the big payment they require each month. If you have a rough month and can't quite come up with that money, many debt management companies won't pay any of your creditors until you pay all of your required payment. During my stint in collections, I saw this regularly. We'd call someone attempting to collect, and all they could tell us is that they were working with CCCS. They couldn't understand why the payment wasn't made on time (and sometimes not at all). This was a very common scenario.

- *Fees*–Even not-for-profit debt management companies expect payment for their services in most cases. With for-profit companies, the fees are all over the board, so I won't even provide an estimate. For not-for-profit agencies, you can expect to spend a couple hundred dollars to get started and about $50 per month thereafter. This is a broad estimate but can give you an idea of what you should expect to spend. If you're drowning in debt, do you have this extra cash?

So what do I suggest? Fight the battles yourself. You can get as good of an interest rate in most cases as someone dealing with a debt management company if you explain and work out your own repayment plan with the creditor. You can often use their built-in forbearance program offerings to your advantage and build your own debt repayment plan. Is it easier? No. Do you have to deal with the hassle? Yes. I've seen debt management companies provide excellent results for their clients, and I've seen others act miserably. I've seen clients succeed, and I've seen clients fail. But I have to go back to the genesis of this book's question about risk. The way I see it is this,–To you are adding a layer of risk and removing yourself from the heat of the fight when you bring in a debt management company. If you want to really beat your debt, you need to be directly involved. Take on your bills on your own, armed with the knowledge of what CCCS can do, and you can probably do as well or better than if you hired them.

Action Steps/Questions

1. I teach that you should avoid Debt Management Companies altogether, instead fighting creditors on your own. Do you agree or disagree with that strategy? Why?

2. What is the primary difference between a for-profit and a not-for-profit debt management company (other than their business classification)?

3. What is the difference in a debt settlement approach and a debt management plan?

Chapter 15:
I Give Up: Bankruptcy

"I told my doctor I broke my leg in two places.
He said 'Stop going to those places.'"

–Henny Youngman

According to the American Bankruptcy Institute, there were a total of 875,635 non-business U.S. bankruptcy filings in 2014 alone. Although that may be a shocking number, in 2010, there were 1,536,799! Bankruptcy has become a common answer for someone who is in debt and just wants to get out. For about $1,000 and a little bit of time, most of your debt can be wiped away for good. This is why most people who file bankruptcy feel like it is a fresh start. And, really, they're not wrong. It is a fresh start. It has been my experience, however, that bankruptcy doesn't solve the real problem–it only alleviates the symptoms for a while. Don't get me wrong–there are benefits for someone who files bankruptcy.

According to the law, once you've been assigned a docket number by the court, your creditors must stop contacting you about any of your debts included in the bankruptcy and must instead contact your attorney (this does not apply if you file pro se, meaning you are representing yourself). This means no more stressful phone calls, no more harassing letters, and an end to most of the headaches associated with those debts. This alone is the biggest reason I believe people file–they just don't know how to handle the headache any longer. They just want it to be over. If you are one of the millions who are contemplating bankruptcy, I hope you will at least understand the process, the pros and cons, and make a decent decision. Too many people have used bankruptcy as their "easy out" when it is rarely the best way.

There are two major types of personal (non-business) bankruptcy that you may be considering: Chapter 7 and Chapter 13. Don't get hung up on the language here – the U.S. Bankruptcy Code (formally called Title 11) is broken down into chapters. Chapters 7 and 13 apply to individuals, while the others apply to specific types of businesses (family farmers and fishermen are covered under Chapter 12, corporate reorganizations are covered under Chapter 11, etc.). These are simply classifications of the bankruptcy code that outline how the process works. Let's look at Chapter 7 first.

Total Liquidation

Chapter 7 bankruptcy is also referred to as "total liquidation." In Chapter 7, you are seeking forgiveness (discharge) of all of your debts, potentially giving up ownership of all your assets that aren't covered by a state or federal exemption. What qualifies as an exempt asset? It depends on the state you live in. For example, in Texas, one of the most bankruptcy-friendly states in the U.S., you can exempt your personal residence (no matter how much it is worth), as well as up to $60,000 worth of personal property (if you are categorized as the head of the household).

Other than exempt assets, a Chapter 7 bankruptcy can place you at risk of losing anything of value. The court will assign a trustee who oversees the bankruptcy process, including the liquidation of all non-exempt assets. He/she has a very wide span of control over your bankruptcy process, so how he/she will approach distributing your assets to cover your debts can vary greatly from case to case. No matter what, someone filing Chapter 7 should expect to give up a lot of his/her assets to pay back debts. Provided the Chapter 7 goes all the way through, any remaining debts after all items of value are liquidated are forgiven (discharged), effectively wiping your financial slate clean and allowing you a fresh start.

Before you get too excited, let's briefly discuss the catch. Certain debts are not eligible for discharge (forgiveness). Child support, alimony, certain types of income/property taxes, and student loans may not be included as a part of the bankruptcy process in 99% of the cases (there are a few exceptions which are very specific to certain situations). So if you have a big student loan debt, don't think you can file bankruptcy to make it go away. You're pretty much guaranteed to be stuck with it until it is fully paid.

You also should know that a Chapter 7 filing will be reported to the credit bureaus and will stay on your report for ten full years from the date of filing. This can and will have a huge negative impact on your credit score, your ability to borrow money, and anything else that relates to your credit report. In addition, if you get into financial troubles again, you are probably stuck for a while. Current law dictates that you cannot file for Chapter 7 bankruptcy for eight years after the last date of filing, effectively putting you on your own for eight years after wiping that slate clean.

If you would like a more detailed look at the Chapter 7 Bankruptcy process, you should review the details provided by the U.S. Courts website, which provides a great deal of detail even in their summary/basics section: *http://www.uscourts.gov/FederalCourts/Bankruptcy/*

BankruptcyBasics/Chapter7.aspx. Warning: This website gives enough detail so that if you thought my summary was boring, you should probably drink a pot of coffee before tackling the website. If you want some more specific information based on the state in which you live, you should check out Legal Consumer, at *http://www. legalconsumer.com.*

The Wage Earner's Plan

A less severe form of bankruptcy for individuals is Chapter 13. Chapter 13 bankruptcy is quite similar to the Corporate Chapter 11 bankruptcy you hear about all the time in the news, as it is purposed to help someone who is capable of repaying most of his/her debts to set up a court-approved repayment plan that fits a reasonable budget and allows them to reorganize their financial life. Under Chapter 13, the debtor proposes a plan to repay his creditors over a 3- to 5-year period instead of the originally-agreed-upon terms. If this detailed plan is approved by the court and the process begins, the debtor gains some breathing room from creditors as he is then only responsible for following the new agreed-upon plan, and creditors cannot attempt to collect past due debts except by action in the bankruptcy court.

For the most part, the person filing Chapter 13 is able to keep his personal property and creditors receive most (but rarely all) of the amount they are owed. This is a much better scenario for creditors in most cases vs. a Chapter 7 filing, in which it is common for creditors to receive nothing. Chapter 13 bankruptcy is really just a more formal version of a debt management plan that we outlined in the chapter on Debt Management and CCCS. Your creditors agree upon a specific interest rate and terms that are more favorable than the original terms and you commit to a specific monthly payment that will satisfy the debt within a given period. The major difference, however, is that a Chapter 13 bankruptcy comes with many legal protections that a debt management plan through a Debt Management Company or CCCS does not offer.

Again, don't get too excited before you learn about the downsides. First and foremost, the majority of Chapter 13 bankruptcy filings fail. Why? Because like every other debt management plan (DMP), you must make payments, and the payments have to adhere strictly to the requirements agreed upon when the repayment plan began. It is true that a Chapter 13 bankruptcy can be converted to a Chapter 7 if payments are no longer being made, and this is actually the most common scenario when payments are no longer affordable for the debtor. You also may not apply for any new credit of any kind during the entire process of the Chapter 13 without the permission of the bankruptcy court. While this may not be a bad thing, it does greatly limit your options at a time when you are likely running very short on cash with possibly no good way to build up a reserve.

The repayment schedule for most Chapter 13 filings is tough because the court closely reviews your budget to determine what it thinks you can afford and sets your repayment terms based on that amount. That is not always friendly to the reality of your situation.

In addition to the challenges mentioned above, if you file Chapter 13, your credit report will reflect the filing for seven years from the completion date (the date you paid your last payment according to the repayment terms, instead of 10 years from the filing date with a Chapter 7), and you cannot file again for two years after the completion date.

If you would like a more detailed look at the Chapter 13 bankruptcy process, review the details provided by the U.S. Courts system. This web page, like the one covering Chapter 7, goes into great detail: *http://www.uscourts. gov/FederalCourts/Bankruptcy/BankruptcyBasics/ Chapter13.aspx*. As I recommended for Chapter 7, if you want some more specific information based on the state in which you live, you should check out Legal Consumer, at *http://www.legalconsumer.com*.

My Thoughts on Bankruptcy

Now that you have some details about how bankruptcy works and what it can/cannot do for you, what is the best course of action if you are buried in debt? First, stop digging! You cannot borrow your way out of debt, and there is no quick or easy way to make your debt go away. You didn't get into debt quickly, and you won't get out quickly either through bankruptcy or any other plan. Are there times where filing bankruptcy is the appropriate answer to a mountain of debt? I believe there is (I know, you're shocked!). An example of this is medical debt. If someone has not heeded my prior warnings about insurance and finds himself with a major illness, it is not unusual that after receiving treatment he will be presented with a huge stack of unpaid bills amounting to hundreds of thousands or even millions of dollars. The average person has no possibility of paying these bills, so bankruptcy might be an option.

If the statistics were easily available, I would be interested in knowing how many bankruptcies were due to true needs vs. someone looking for an easy out (and I know it would be a judgment call for each case), but you and I both can agree that bankruptcy is an abused method of doing away with debt. The Bible says in Psalm 37:21

that "the wicked borrow and do not repay…" and I firmly believe that statement. You should never use bankruptcy as an escape from your debts when there is any possibility of your being able to repay them.

If you're in major trouble with debt, I'd highly recommend you set up an appointment with a competent, well-trained financial counselor before you meet with a bankruptcy attorney. The bankruptcy attorney is much more likely to advise you to file Chapter 7 or 13 because that's what he does. A good financial counselor will consider your situation and be up front and honest about what he sees. Maybe bankruptcy is the right choice–but don't make that call too early. How can you find a good counselor in your area? You have a couple of good options:

1. Contact me at *http://www.humoroushomemaking.com/ financial-coaching.* I provide one-on-one financial coaching for a fee. Depending on your situation, we can meet in person, by telephone, or through Skype or some other technology that allows interaction.

2. Visit *http://www.daveramsey.com* and click on "financial coaching." Dave has a network of coaches he endorses, and if they're good enough for Dave to endorse, they're good enough for me to recommend.

No matter what you do, don't wait until you're so far into your mess of debt that you feel like bankruptcy is your only option. It could mean thousands of dollars wasted and months of unnecessary time spent worrying and struggling to pursue the wrong solutions.

1. Many people believe bankruptcy is evil, while others believe it is a fresh start. In which camp do you fall and why?

2. For how long should you expect your credit bureau report to be negatively impacted if you file Chapter 7 bankruptcy?

3. For how long should you expect your credit bureau report to be negatively impacted if you file Chapter 13 bankruptcy?

Chapter 16:
Tying it All Together

"Whether you think that you can, or that you can't, you are usually right."

–Henry Ford

Well, there you have it. We've gone over a full range of topics on debt including a real-world definition of what debt is, how it works, and what you can do to rid yourself of it. I hope you took notes and went through the exercises and questions I provided. If you didn't, please don't put this book down until you go back and review those questions/exercises at the end of each chapter and at least mentally answer them. Some of them may seem silly, even to the point of ridiculous. I don't know what your specific issue or situation is, but we are all ignorant of certain topics and we have all been misinformed about others. Even if you feel you are an expert on a certain chapter, recognize that your friends and/or family may be struggling with that very topic. You should be ready to help them. I encourage you to share your knowledge and empower others to move from debtor to better.

Debt is a big and scary creature that way too many people are battling. If you will implement the suggestions I provide in this book and battle debt with the weapons of knowledge I've given you, you will win. You won't have it easy and your progress won't be without setbacks, but you can beat the monster of debt. You can move from being a debtor, enslaved to the bills that arrive in your mailbox each month, to being better, freed from the chains your debt has you in. I'm a living example that debt doesn't have to be a part of your life, and let me tell you, friend: Freedom feels good.

Will you join me in the ranks of those who have decided debt is stupid? Will you sacrifice and fight your way out of debt to be able to taste the victory of actually owning your stuff? Will you be smart with your money now so that later you can go out to dinner and give your server, the single mom who is trying to make ends meet, a $100 tip because you know it will help and you actually can afford to help? Will you show your kids what it means to be responsible with money? Will you show your spouse that you really do love him or her and care about your relationship enough to communicate about money? Will you stop wasting time reading my motivational speech and get to it already!? GO! Why are you still reading!? GO! Your future depends on it.

Afterword

When I started writing this book, I started out just thinking I'd write a brief summary of the various aspects of debt that I deal with regularly and offer my thoughts on how to handle each of them. But as I built the outline and developed my thoughts, I realized how big this debt monster really is! I purposefully did not tackle subjects such as student loan debt, issues of divorce, repossession, foreclosure, judgments, etc. I could have kept writing and filled dozens more pages with ease. But I chose to stop before this book got too big for you to be willing to read it. I also need fodder for future books!

I truly hope that you have found reading this book a valuable learning experience that has given you insight into the world of debt and how you can free yourself from its clutches. As you go forward and conquer your debt challenges, I hope you will share your stories of success and provide suggestions on what I should include in future editions of *From Debtor to Better*. Contact me at *http://www.humoroushomemaking.com*. I wish you all the best and thank you for investing in your financial success by buying this book.

About the Author

Barry Myers is a financial coach gifted with the ability to provide practical, real-world solutions to positively impact people where it often matters most–their pocketbooks. His approach looks beyond the simple math of personal finance to place the focus on the behavior that drives financial choices. Using proven principles and  old-fashioned common sense, Barry helps people get out of debt, save for short- and long-term goals, and set good priorities with their money.

Barry holds an M.B.A., along with a Bachelor of Science in Business and Accounting. He is a regular speaker at conferences, workshops, and other events. He also partners with his wife to run Humorous Homemaking (*http://www.humoroushomemaking.com*), a community dedicated to helping families run their homes without losing their minds.

Barry offers custom-tailored workshops for businesses, schools, and churches, as well as one-on-one financial coaching sessions. He also acts as a keynote speaker at conferences, business meetings, and other similar events.

Appendix

Helpful References and Recommended Resources

Income Sources Worksheet

Source	$ Amount	How Often Received	Monthly $ Amount	Notes
Salary 1				
Salary 2				
Salary 3				
Bonus				
Commission				
Self-Employment				
Dividend Income				
Royalty Income				
Rents				
Notes				
Alimony				
Child Support				
Unemployment				
Social Security				
Pension				
Annuity				
Disability				
Cash Gifts				
Trust Fund				
Other				
Other				
Other				
Other				
TOTAL				

Irregular Bills Worksheet

Bill	$ Amount	How Often Paid	Monthly $ Amount	Notes
Real Estate Taxes				
Homeowners Ins.				
Home Repairs				
Replace Furniture				
Medical Bills (Rx, etc.)				
Health Insurance				
Life Insurance				
Disability Insurance				
Car Insurance				
Car Repair/Replace				
Car Tags/Taxes				
Clothing (special)				
Tuition				
Bank Note				
IRS (Self-Employed)				
Vacation				
Gifts (special)				
Other				
Other				
Other				
Other				
Other				
Other				
TOTAL				

Monthly Bills Worksheet

Bill	$ Amount	Due Date	Notes
Total from Irregulars			
TOTAL			

Cash Flow Calendar

Sunday	Monday	Tuesday	Wednesday	Thursday	Friday	Saturday

Cash Flow Calendar (Example)

Sunday	Monday	Tuesday	Wednesday	Thursday	Friday	Saturday
	1 +900: paycheck -120: charity -400: rent	**2** -80: entertainment -35: gifts -25: clothing/shoes	**3**	**4**	**5** -30: gas -80: groceries	**6**
7	**8**	**9**	**10**	**11**	**12** -30: gas -80: groceries	**13**
14	**15** +900: paycheck -120: charity -50: home improvement	**16** -100: electricity -30: water/sewer/trash -100: car maintenance*	**17** -25: clothing/shoes	**18**	**19** -30: gas -80: groceries	**20**
21	**22**	**23** -50: phone/internet	**24**	**25** -40: cell phone	**26** -30: gas -80: groceries	**27**
28 -100: savings -25: car insurance*	**29**	**30**	**31**			

* - money to be set aside for irregular bill

Categorized Budget (Example)

Category	$ Amount Budgeted	$ Remaining
Net Income	$ 1800	$ 1800
Charitable Giving	240	1560
Personal Savings	100	1460
Food	320	1140
Mortgage/Rent	400	740
Auto Fuel	120	620
Auto Insurance (pay monthly)	25	595
Water/Sewer/Trash	30	565
Electricity	100	465
Clothing and Shoes	50	415
Home Improvement/Maintenance	50	365
Entertainment	80	285
Auto Maintenance and Replacement	100	185
Miscellaneous Household	40	145
Home Telephone	25	120
Cell Phone	40	80
Internet	25	55
Gifts	35	20
Unallocated (extra or additional debt repayment)	20	$ 0

Sample Credit Report Dispute Letter

To file a dispute by mail, simply copy the content of this letter, modifying any sections in {} and send to the appropriate reporting agency's address.

{DATE}
{YOUR NAME}
{YOUR ADDRESS}
{CITY, STATE, ZIP CODE}

{COMPANY NAME}
{COMPANY ADDRESS}
{CITY, STATE, ZIP CODE}

Dear Sir or Madam:

I recently obtained a copy of my credit report from your company and found the following to be in error:

Item 1: I dispute {XYZ CREDIT CARD}, account number {XXXXXXXXXX}. {REASON FOR DISPUTE}.

I am requesting that the item be {REMOVED, UPDATED, CHANGED} to correct the information.

Enclosed are copies of {DOCUMENTATION} supporting my position. Please reinvestigate this (these) matter(s) and correct the disputed item(s) as soon as possible.

Sincerely,

{YOUR NAME}

Recommended Websites

- www.humoroushomemaking.com – The website my wife and I run to teach others how to manage their homes without losing their minds. You can find numerous articles on personal finance topics and learn more about our family.

- www.daveramsey.com - Basic Budgeting, Personal Finance and Debt Reduction

- www.mint.com – Personal money-management site with lots of free tools

- www.javacalc.com – Numerous online calculators for everything from debt reduction to retirement planning

- www.mymoney.gov – Federal-government-run site covering basic personal finance topics with some free calculators and planning tools

- www.crown.org – Basic Budgeting, Personal Finance and Debt Reduction

Recommended Books

- *48 Days to the Work You Love* by Dan Miller

- *No More Dreaded Mondays* by Dan Miller

- *The Total Money Makeover* by Dave Ramsey

- *Money Matters* by Larry Burkett

- *The Millionaire Next Door* by Thomas Stanley

- *Thou Shalt Prosper* by Daniel Lapin

- *Smart Money Smart Kids* by Dave Ramsey and Rachel Cruze

Made in the USA
Columbia, SC
11 March 2019